William Bloom PhD has been running workshops on psychic protection for over twenty years. He is one of Britain's most influential teachers in the new age approach to life. He is the author of several books, including *Meditation in a Changing World* and *Money, Heart and Mind*.

Praise for Psychic Protection:

Gives you the power to change the atmosphere around you so that you can deliver your best . . . gives techniques that can be used when you know you are going into a difficult situation . . . whether it's a difficult business meeting, handling a family row or coping with road rage.

Daily Mail

Gives support and tools that are of excellent quality, navigation aids that will keep you safe on your journey and encourage you to settle for nothing less than your best . . . essential reading in today's world.

Caduceus **magazine**

Contains some brilliant breathing and grounding techniques which made me feel so calm and relaxed that nothing could have bothered me. *Here's Health*

Finally a masculine voice speaking in a heart-centred way about the intuitive. This is an important guide for those who seek to be both grounded and spiritually connected.

Julia Cameron, author of *The Artist's Way*

A rather special book . . . genuine and sincere . . . William Bloom has covered a complex, comprehensive subject with skill and expertise which has obviously demanded much deep thinking. The book is written with a great deal of regard to the individual's needs. The mere act of reading it is likely to engender feelings of love, compassion and a sense of peace.

From affording oneself with personal protection, to having a positive effect on the rest of the world, this book is a must for everybody — not just those who are interested in matters of the life of the metaphysical. A superior book of its kind. *Horoscope* **magazine**

PSYCHIC
PROTECTION

PSYCHIC
PROTECTION

Creating Positive Energies for
People and Places

William Bloom

PIATKUS

For Eileen Caddy

First published in 1996 by
Judy Piatkus (Publishers) Ltd
5 Windmill Street, London W1P 1HF

Reprinted 1996, 1997, 1998 (twice)

The moral right of the author has been asserted

A catalogue record for this book is
available from the British Library

ISBN 0-7499-1603-6

Edited by Carol Franklin
Designed by Sue Ryall
Artwork by Zena Flax

Set in Imprint and Helvetica
by Computerset, Harmondsworth
Printed and bound in Great Britain by
Biddles Ltd, Guildford and King's Lynn

Contents

1

The background

What's the issue?

'I have this friend who just completely drains me. Every time I see her I come away feeling that I have no energy for anything.'

'I'm about to move into a new home and I don't like the house's atmosphere.'

'When I go into business meetings I feel intimidated by the atmosphere and I freeze.'

'We had these people stay in the flat and we really did not like the atmosphere they left behind.'

'I have this one client and after he has left I feel as if I have some of him stuck to me.'

'There is this person who hates me and I keep feeling that their thoughts are inside my head.'

'I live in the country and when I visit the city, I get overwhelmed by the vibrations.'

'I'm completely drained by travelling in the rush-hour underground.'

These are common problems. They are caused by our natural sensitivity to energies and atmospheres. To one degree or another everyone is sensitive to the atmosphere of places, objects and people. Entering a church or library, we may feel its serenity. We like particular houses because they feel good and avoid others because they feel bad. Even the most cynical of people may enter a meeting or a bar and sense immediately whether the environment is hostile or friendly. People also feel the moods of different landscapes. Atmospheres can dramatically affect how you feel and behave, without your being conscious of them. This book is dedicated to liberating you from these unseen influences and giving you the opportunity to live more consciously and creatively.

For a fulfilled and healthy life it is crucial to be able to understand and work with the vibrations which affect you, both to protect yourself and to change them. It has long been accepted in psychology that a basic need of all people is to feel both physically and psychologically safe. If you do not feel safe, it is difficult to behave with dignity, joy and creativity and to fulfil your potential. Psychic protection, therefore, makes sense for all of us. It serves no one to feel vulnerable and unable to control their emotions in new, difficult or negative atmospheres. We all need to feel confident and empowered.

This book has been written for everyone who is sensitive to atmospheres and who would like to do something creative and helpful about them. You may be a full-time parent or business person, a teacher or a salesperson, a professional carer or a plumber, a computer operator or a gardener. Whatever you do, though, you have to work with people and in places – and sometimes you will want to know the practical strategies for creatively changing atmospheres. It is no help to you or anyone else if you are wobbled off centre by particular people, situations or places, and lose your ability to behave to your and other people's best advantage. Equally, it will serve you, your family, your colleagues and your friends in general if you also know how to create an atmosphere that helps everyone deliver their best.

In the past many societies had specialists – shamans, medicine people, mystical priests and priestesses, exorcists and so on – who understood and practised the art of changing atmospheres and creating psychic protection. My experience is, however, that almost anyone can do this 'energy work'. The techniques are very straightforward and there is no need for knowledge about them to be kept secret or shrouded in mystery. These techniques also require no special skills or gadgets, so it is possible to practice them without being embarrassingly visible.

In this book I share these basic strategies in a way that is easy to learn and to put into practice. They require no special background knowledge or attitude so if you are completely new to this kind of information do not worry. It is all very easily learned. These techniques also do not require a great deal of time or effort. Once you understand them you will see that they are very natural, like swimming or riding a bicycle or dancing or reading.

You will also find that you can use them in all kinds of ordinary and particularly challenging situations: meetings with new or important people, in irritated post office queues, traffic jams, bars, streets at night, with angry relatives – all kinds of situations that you meet in everyday life.

The main skills I have been teaching, and which you will find explained in this book, are listed below:

- how to maintain your own psychic space in uncomfortable or intimidating situations;
- how to protect yourself against powerful personalities and against people whose energy and attitude affect you;
- how to maintain your own energy field without external interference;

- how to cleanse your home or workplace;
- how to settle the atmosphere after a row or guests, or an unwelcome situation;
- how to create a benevolent and loving vibration which you can then place in an object or space;
- how to create a general attitude and lifestyle that is energetically beneficial.

My aim is that by the end of this book, whatever your background, you will feel confident that you understand and can put these techniques into effective practice.

Let me give right here a very simple example of this kind of work. You may, for instance, be given a jumper you like, but you are not happy with its atmosphere because of where it has been or from whom it comes. What can you do?

The answer is easy. Vibrate the jumper rigorously, shake it about, put it on the floor and jump on it, bash it around. This will shake out the old vibration and leave it neutral. A good wash or dry clean will also work.

Psychologically, of course, this helps you to perceive the object in a new way, free of past associations. *Vibrationally*, however, you have genuinely shaken up its actual atomic structure so as to release the atmosphere held in it.

Here is another very simply example. Vibration and shaking can also be used on yourself. For example, if you come out of a meeting and feel that you have absorbed and are holding on to other people's 'stuff', all you need to do is just give your body and clothes a good long shake. This will usually be enough to remove it. You will find more on this in Chapter 3.

My personal background

I know how easy it is to do this kind of work because I have been doing it myself for 30 years and teaching it for 20.

The main reason I became involved in all of this is because since infancy, like many people, I have been very sensitive to atmospheres. I remember being taken to nursery school and noticing alleyways that felt frightening. Playing in the park there were certain areas and trees that I wanted to avoid. Most embarrassing, I remember being frightened of the long dark corridor of the flat in which we lived. I deliberately avoided walking down it to go to the lavatory and, instead, peed – at the age of two and three – behind the curtains in the sitting room. The strangest thing of all is that no one in the family ever mentioned it. Perhaps, if they noticed, they thought it was the cat.

You will be glad to know that I have overcome that particular fear (I can be safely invited into your home) and that I no longer take long distance jumps on to my bed in order to avoid the strange monster with groping hands. Nevertheless I have continued to be disturbed by atmosphere.

The whole lifestyle and way of thinking of my family led me to believe that my sensitivity was just the result of an overactive imagination. I therefore kept very quiet about most of my sensitivities and anxieties. If I did express my anxiety about a certain object or place I would either be laughed at because it was 'unmanly' or comforted with a genuinely caring cuddle and the statement, 'There, there, don't worry, there's nothing there.' But the irony is that, in fact, there *was* something there.

There was often an unpleasant atmosphere which I could distinctly feel, but my mother, who loved me and truly wanted to comfort me, was behaving like a million other parents. I was comforted and told there was nothing there. This is a strange situation, isn't it? Genuine care joined with sincere ignorance. The result for me, and for many other people, is a certain confusion and even some shame about our sensitivity. It is still occasionally embarrassing for me, especially if confronted by authoritarian sceptics, to talk openly about these things.

I therefore always encourage parents to take the sensitivities of children more seriously. If a child is anxious, she of course still needs comfort, but instead of saying that there's nothing there, parents might say something like, 'OK, let's have a look and feel of what is there. How does it really feel to you? Tell me about it. Maybe we can do something about it.'

As I grew older and went into my teens and then early twenties, my ability to feel vibrations never left me. I was also quite tough, smoking and drinking, and riding a large motorbike. I may have been sensitive to vibrations, but I was not generally sensitive or poetic. In fact, my personality was harsh. My impressions of people and places, however, were very clear and powerful. I could tell immediately what kind of a mood someone was in regardless of the front they were projecting, and I found new houses and landscapes fascinating precisely because of the changes in atmosphere.

When I was about 22, I began to meditate – as a survival mechanism in a stressful job – and I found my sensitivity increasing. It increased simply because I was sitting quietly. With my emotions and thoughts relaxed, there was less 'interference', less 'noise' and I became more open and aware of what I was actually experiencing in my body and energy field. Equally important, sitting quietly every day, I became acutely aware of the kind of atmosphere that I myself was creating. These atmospheres, I noticed, were entirely dependent upon my moods. I reached the startling personal conclusion that by deliberately changing my mood I could distinctly affect how a place or a person felt.

Having realised this, I must admit to having used it mischievously a few times. Late at night, telling spooky stories to friends, I would also put myself into a spooky mood, and watched with glee while my friends became temporarily frightened. I also began to experiment with creating a benevolent atmosphere and I became increasingly aware of what a powerful force for good – and bad – this natural human ability is. There are energy bullies, for instance, who push their weight around by intimidating people with their vibrations – I am sure that most people have encountered someone like this.

Around the same time I began reading all kinds of books on mysticism, spiritual psychology and the occult. Many of these books discussed how human beings can affect and manipulate energy and atmospheres. It did not take much thought to realise that it was important to make a clear moral decision about my attitude to this energy work and I did: I am only interested in energy work if it is of loving benefit. In fact, at 25, I took 2 years' spiritual retreat in the mountains of Southern Morocco to commit myself more fully to this path and to learn more about the actual methods for moving and changing energy (see my book *The Sacred Magician*, Gothic Image Publishers).

Those two years of retreat were a time of intense learning for me and, when I returned to London, I began to use my new awareness and skills to help change atmospheres that were frightening and bothering. Most people I met were disturbed by energy problems which, if they only knew the basic skills, they could deal with themselves. (The most common two problems were living in a house with an uncomfortable atmosphere or feeling frightened and affected by someone else's emotions and thoughts.) So what really began to interest me was helping people to learn these basic energy skills so that they could get on with their lives more confidently and creatively. The actual teaching began in a very casual way. I would, for instance, meet someone or a group of people who were being disturbed by an atmosphere in their house or workplace and I would get into conversation with them. During the conversation I would share my ideas on how they might deal with the situation and they were usually interested in my expertise and grateful. They then might send a friend with similar problems to see me. This happened to me many times.

Then visiting the Findhorn Foundation, a spiritual community in Scotland, there were many people interested in my perspective and I was invited to teach classes on the subject. As a result of this I gained the reputation of being useful in this area and I had to begin teaching formal classes in order to avoid the growing requests for one-to-one tutorials. What was always interesting was that the people asking for help were very varied, from every conceivable social and work background: wealthy aristocrats to penniless hippies, medical doctors and nurses to engineers and architects, the occasional priest and nun, plumbers and secretaries and social workers, computer engineers, therapists, full-time parents and pensioners. Over 20 years I have taught these classes mainly at Findhorn and in London, but also internationally in the United States and Western and Eastern Europe.

I have also been particularly touched and encouraged by the feedback. Many people have told me how they at last now feel comfortable in their homes and offices, how they now have a new confidence to deal with previously worrying relationships and work situations. Personally what touches me the most is the feedback from people who have carried anxiety for most of their lives and now find that they are feeling generally more comfortable and generous. Having a doctorate in psychology and having worked with many psychotherapies, I am very aware of the psychological realities that underlie insecurity, fear and anxiety. As an energy worker, though, as someone who is sensitive to invisible atmospheres and vibrations, I also know that the problem is often not psychological but energetic. Techniques of psychic protection, therefore, and strategies for creating positive energies can substantially reassure and empower us without the need for deeper psychological work. This is good news for all of us.

The underlying dynamics

If we are dealing with atmospheres and vibrations, then we have to expand our usual way of understanding life.

Everything that exists in a material form which we can see and touch also has a more subtle energy body that we cannot see. This is clear enough in modern physics: every

Objects and their energy fields

atom is made up of dancing energy. There are also photographic processes, such as Kirlian, which can actually photograph these energy fields.

These energy fields are capable of containing and radiating particular qualities of atmosphere. These atmospheres vary enormously, from peace to anger, from joy to sadness, from anxiety to confidence, and so on. These different atmospheres not only sit in solid forms – for instance, the brickwork of a house – but they also float in the air. They float in the air and they move around to different places and to different people. When someone has a tantrum, the energy and atmosphere of the tantrum may float way beyond the person actually having it and be felt by someone else a great distance away. Many people have experiences of suddenly knowing that a close friend or relative is in a certain mood. Equally, many people often have a sense that someone is thinking about them. One of the features of being in love is the feeling of being connected by emotions even when the lovers are separated. You may also sense the raging thoughts of an enemy.

In a very real sense, all of this follows a basic law of the physical world which is that energy never disappears. When people, for instance, feel anger or joy they put energy into this feeling and this energy continues. It may sit quietly in their body, perhaps causing ongoing tension in the stomach, or it may be released beyond the body into the air (see illustration). Whatever happens to it, it continues to exist in some form or another. It may float around in the larger energy field of the person who first felt it; it may become absorbed by that person's house or workplace; it may land on someone else who might then hold on to it or release it with more feeling. We will be returning to this subject later in the book.

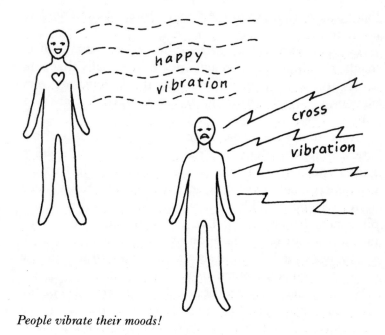

People vibrate their moods!

Perception and discrimination

As you become involved in this work you will find that there is the huge problem of whether you are accurately sensing and perceiving these realities, or whether you are just imagining them. This goes hand in hand with confusion about how you actually do the perceiving. There are some people who see pictures and get images, others who hear sounds or smell scents; while others talk about intuition and direct knowing.

In actual fact, the way that most of us perceive atmospheres and vibrations is through feeling and sensing them. I am not talking about an emotional feeling, but about something that is more of a physical sensation. You can sense and feel atmospheres and vibrations in the same way that you feel changes in the temperature, or dampness, or a breeze.

The main experience of atmospheres does not take place inside the brain and imagination. It actually happens across the whole body. Sometimes the feelings are very obvious, even overwhelming, and sometimes they are very subtle.

Every human being has an energy field which is not only interwoven with their material physical body but which also extends beyond it. Every one of us has an electromagnetic energy field extending several feet, sometimes much more, beyond us. This energy field is made up of our physical radiance and vitality, and is also made up of the radiance of our emotions and thoughts. This energy field, sometimes called the aura, is also created by the radiance of our general consciousness.

Some readers may not be familiar with the idea of the aura because it is not taught in western biology or medicine. It is however a basic concept in oriental and Ayurvedic medicine, and is certainly not a strange idea in the light of modern science which understands that everything is made up of energy. It is an important part of everybody's bio-energetic make-up and it is important that we know about it if we are to understand how psychic protection and creating positive energies actually work.

The aura is an electromagnetic energy field which passes all the way through the human body and radiates beyond it. Although we cannot see it, we can experience what it is feeling. It is precisely the sensitivity of the aura and how it merges with our nervous system which allows us to feel atmospheres and vibrations. When something vibrates in the aura, we sense it.

Our aura is continually meeting other energy fields and when it meets another field, a wobble or wave is sent through it, like when a pebble falls into water. This vibration then anchors down through the skin into the physical nervous system. The brain notices the sensation in the nervous system and then interprets the experience. This is incredibly obvious when, for example, you meet something like an angry dog which frightens you. Your energy field meets the energy of the angry dog and there is that wobble or friction where they meet. This wobble travels through your energy field and lands in the nervous system down the spine and your spinal hair literally stands on end. Your brain then interprets this experience: fear.

The same thing happens when we meet a benevolent person or place. Our energy field encounters their benevolent energy field. The harmonic where they meet is communicated down into the physical nervous system and it feels good.

This is also exactly what happens when we go into the countryside or a building. Harmonious landscape, for example near moving water or underground springs, is felt by our energy body. Beautiful landscape is not just perceived by our eyes but is felt by the whole body. This is why so many people from cities want to spend time in the country, feeling and absorbing the nurturing atmosphere of landscape.

As we enter new buildings, we also often immediately feel the quality of the place. Our aura meets the general vibration of the building. Anyone looking around for a new home knows the experience of a place simply feeling bad even if it looks great. And sometimes we find houses and apartments which look terrible but have a great atmosphere. The house in which I am writing this book looked terrible when we moved in, but it had a wonderful warm family atmosphere.

There are nevertheless genuine difficulties in being accurate about what we are sensing. We carry our own vibrations around with us and there may be many situations in which we feel something and think it is external, coming from, say, a building, when in fact the vibrations are coming from within us. We may also, for various reasons to do with history and temperament, react to something intensely and think that it is negative, when in fact it is harmless. A frequent example is if you meet someone who has a threatening image, like a sullen male teenager. He may, in fact, be the sweetest kid just dressing like his peers, but his image is enough to trigger your own fear. You feel 'hostile vibrations' but they are in fact all yours.

All through this book, therefore, I shall be cautioning you to be aware of projections and stuff that belong to your own psyche and I will explain the psychological dynamics that can interfere with accurate perception.

You can never guarantee that your inner impressions are accurate. You, therefore, need to be open and receptive to impressions, without your concrete mind blocking the process, but at the same time you need to maintain a healthy scepticism. This requires an attitude of inner amusement, not taking it all too seriously, an openness to being wrong – and at the same time a reborn childishness that is open and receptive to new sensations and images.

Generally speaking, if an inner impression is accurate, then it will sit comfortably and wisely in you. If the inner impression causes you some excitement, then you will have to wait until you have calmed down to feel whether or not it still rings true. You will find more on this in different parts of this book.

Becoming an active player

Taking atmospheres seriously and knowing the basic techniques for working with them is empowering and confidence-building. Instead of being a passive unconscious player in this world of energies and vibrations, you can become an active player directly influencing and controlling your environment.

This is why I have such enthusiasm for energy work. I believe that the whole purpose of human life is for our true essence – unique to each of us – to shine through, for each of us to become who we truly are and genuinely fulfil ourselves.

But to fulfil ourselves we need certain basic conditions. We obviously need food and shelter and physical safety. But as mentioned earlier, and worth stressing again, we also need psychological safety. And we need to feel that we have self-control. We cannot fulfil ourselves if we have no influence over the energies and atmospheres which may continually influence us where we live and work and play.

This energy work of protection, cleansing and blessing helps us feel less afraid and more confident. People who begin to experiment with energy work are often astonished by the psychological benefits that it brings them. There can be huge relief as they lose their sense of vulnerability and lack of control.

I also believe that our sensitivity and our ability to work with atmospheres is completely natural. Cynics, sceptics and religious fundamentalists may attack energy work as superstitious, unintelligent or even the work of the devil. For me these people are like the flat earthers of several centuries ago. They are out of date. They are missing reality.

As well as being for your own personal benefit, this inner work can be very beneficial for your family, friends, workplaces and colleagues, in fact for all the different communities in which you live and participate. To clean up and nurture the atmosphere in your homes and workplaces is a real service. Working in a more disciplined and sustained way, it is also possible to clear up the atmosphere in your neighbourhoods. This may sound extravagant, but I have experienced this in reality over and over again.

Later in the book I will describe exactly how you can work in this way. You will see that it is genuinely possible and already practised by many people who enjoy this aspect of the work because it gives them a real sense of doing something useful for the world. Alongside the physical pollution which is challenging the ecology of our planet, there is also a great deal of vibrational pollution made up of negative attitudes, feelings and thoughts. It is possible to work helpfully to clean up this inner environment so as to benefit what we might call the 'psychic ecology' or 'inner ecology', the ecology of vibrations and atmospheres in our planet.

It does not require a great stretch of the imagination to realise the huge amount of invisible psychic pollution that is floating around the whole planet. You can work actively to transform and heal this pollution. At the very least you can take care not to create more. Some people believe indeed that it is this attitudinal and energy pollution which is the root cause of the actual environmental pollution and toxins. Any work that helps to relieve this situation is obviously useful.

The simplest help is just to be a calm oasis of goodwill in the midst of modern craziness. Everyone knows people who radiate a friendly and peaceful presence. I remember an extraordinary tea lady in one place where I worked. Always working against deadlines, there was frequently an atmosphere of stress and people suffering strokes and heart attacks, but at 11 o'clock along would come this benevolent creature dispensing a friendly smile, a cup of tea or coffee and good vibrations.

Inside modern hospitals I often wonder how much of the healing achieved is actually due to the support staff and cleaners who wander around, doing their work with a calm and beneficent attitude.

Good vibrations can actually be measured with scientific instruments. Our brains emit different frequency transmissions – alpha waves, beta waves and so on – according to the level of our relaxation and well-being, which can be scientifically monitored. This technology has been successfully used for stress control and also in the relief of epilepsy. When I was working with special needs students, I met an American tutor who had spent some time researching teaching literacy to adults. The greatest successes came with tutors who radiated a very calm atmosphere, which provided a safe space in which the student could relax, 'unfreeze' the brain and learn. This was actually measured. The tutors with the best vibrations achieved the greatest successes with anxious under-achieving students.

The benefits, personal and collective, of this energy work are clear. Far from being a superstitious diversion for cranks, it is a very sensible approach to life which can provide a confident isle of sanity in an increasingly complex world.

Sympathy for the criticisms

There are many sceptics and critics of this work. 'This is actually all a load of superstitious rubbish. The only reason you believe in it is because you can't face the idea of a world that is beyond your control. So you pretend you can control it.'

In one form or another I have heard these criticisms many times and in a way I am sympathetic to them. The world is full of psychic charlatans and tricksters who will do anything to make money or manipulate people for some kind of personal power trip. Every few months there is a story in our newspapers about some tragedy created by a self-inflated and dangerous guru or psychic master.

Historically it was even worse. In the Middle Ages in

Europe, superstitious trickery was part and parcel of Christian culture, especially in the Church itself. Superstition and spooks reigned supreme. Chicken bones were sold as saints' relics (their fingers) for protection. In fact, almost anything was sold to protect people from the devil and save their souls. Around every corner you could find someone prepared to cast a spell that would in some way or another affect the atmosphere or energies – for success, for victory, for love, for money, for good looks. In many ways organised religion was a part of this racket.

In the 1600s and 1700s, European culture began finally to ditch these absurd and unpleasant beliefs. Quite rightly there are many people today who are frightened of returning to those dark ages and every time they hear about something that resembles medieval superstition, they have a knee-jerk reaction of distrust. I am happy that these people exist for it would be a dangerous world without healthy sceptics.

Academic anthropologists in particular claim that we – like the tribal 'primitive' peoples – make up this inner world of energy so that we can pretend to control that which is uncontrollable. This attitude to the natural wisdom of tribal peoples and to our own general sensitivity is intellectual snobbery at its most narrow-minded. If something does not fit into the contemporary scientific understanding of the universe, then it is deemed childish imagination. But science itself is moving forward now and coming to a more fluid understanding of nature and the cosmos, in which there is a continuum between consciousness and matter, and an understanding that everything is made up of energy in different forms.

There is, however, a more practical difficulty when it comes to believing in energy work. It really is a matter of experience. If you have not experienced it, why should you believe it? We have five obvious senses – touch, taste, scent, sound and sight – which deal with a solid physical world.

We cannot miss the information that they feed through to us. The sixth sense is more subtle, less obvious, but it also is always at work.

Perhaps we tend to ignore this sixth sense simply because we are never taught about it or encouraged to take it seriously. It was not on my school curriculum and my parents never introduced me to it. I wish, in fact, that as a boy I had been taught that sensitivity to vibrations and energy work is normal. It is a completely natural part of life. Awareness of it can bring you nothing but benefits.

2

Earth, body and breath

Safely in your body

To do effective energy work, to change and influence atmospheres, you must be fully in your physical body and you must feel that your body is firmly connected to the earth. You must also be able to breathe in a tranquil and controlled manner. If you are not in your body and earthed, if you cannot breathe calmly, then your perceptions will tend to be inaccurate, and you will have difficulty staying calm in intense and difficult situations.

If I ask a group I am teaching, 'How much are you in your body? How comfortable are you in your physical body? Are you generally aware of your body? Where is the main focus of your attention: in your body, your imagination, your thoughts or feelings?', I receive a large variety of answers.

People come from different backgrounds, have very different histories and are different types. We are all familiar with the poetic type of person whose consciousness seems to be hardly in their body at all. It is as if they are always floating around outside their heads. There are intellectual types who are very busy inside their heads and you can almost sense the energy of their intense thinking processes. Then there are other people who are emotionally stuck and it seems that their energy is clogged in their throats, their voices thin and whispery.

All of these are wide generalisations. What I want you to pick up on is the idea that your consciousness and natural minute-by-minute awareness may not be fully in the whole of your body. In fact, it is rare for modern adults to be comfortably and fully in their bodies. Compare adults with the natural body awareness of children. Young children are physically graceful, balanced and relaxed. Compare us also with tribal peoples or people who work on the land and with their hands; most of us are not using our bodies and are therefore not fully in them.

It would be useful if you stopped for a moment and assessed how much you are in your body. Where are you focused in your body and where are you not focused? This is not a complicated self-assessment, just a small piece of sensing the kind of person you are. *How much are you in your body?*

Let me now ask a second question: *How well grounded are you?* How much are you in touch with the earth beneath you? Do you feel a connection with the physical planet whose gravity holds you and stops you flying off into space? Some people are naturally well grounded, especially those working with their hands or on the land. Most modern people, however, are not well earthed.

And now a third and equally important question: *Is your breath calm and rhythmic?* Or is it jagged, tight and uncomfortable?

These three questions, concerning your body, grounding and breath are crucial. It does not matter how disciplined, focused or experienced you are in using your imagination, if you are not grounded and calm, your energy work will be difficult and inaccurate.

I have worked with many people whose most important

lesson was just to ground themselves. I can think immediately, for instance, of several schoolteachers and business people who were getting increasingly overwhelmed by the atmosphere of their work places. Learning to stay grounded, in their bodies and with a calm breath was all, in fact, that they needed to become comfortable.

Why are body, earth and breath so important? The answer is very practical. It is simply impossible to deal well with life if you are spaced out, anxious and not fully in your body and on the earth. Imagine any threatening or intense situation. To deal with it effectively, you must stay calm and focused. To be calm and focused, your whole physical body needs to be relaxed and stable. If you are focused up in your head or your consciousness is trying to escape the situation, then your body behaves nervously and anxiously. If your body is behaving anxiously, then, of course, it is impossible to feel all right.

Your body is a biological creature and it is also the vehicle of your consciousness. It needs you, your consciousness, to be firmly in the driving seat in order to guide it. If in situations of threat, your consciousness is not firmly in your body but slipping off into panicky psychological states, then your body will experience anxiety. The anxiety triggers a flow of adrenalin and the instinct for the three 'f's: fright, flight or fight. If, on the other hand, you are calmly in your body, then you will have self-control, even over your adrenalin flow.

Calm in the face of threat

Stop for a moment and picture a situation that frightens you. Now imagine yourself in that situation, standing firmly and breathing calmly. You are comfortably in your body. Your face, chest and stomach are relaxed. You are aware of your connection with the earth. Your breathing is relaxed.

You should be able to sense and imagine immediately how that degree of physical self-control can transform the whole way that you experience the situation.

You will easily recognise when you are fully grounded and calmly in your body. The centre of gravity of your body energy will actually sit somewhere around your lower belly. If you watch very young children moving, they have perfect poise and body energy distribution. A toddler can fall backwards directly on to her bottom while her spine stays erect, precisely because her centre of gravity is so low.

Pregnant women have a centre of gravity in their lower belly, so if you have ever been pregnant you may want to remember that sensation without the actual physical weight or fatigue.

Practitioners of Eastern martial arts and movement have

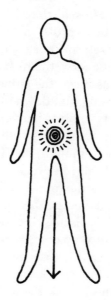

Your physical centre of gravity is in the lower belly

their body energy perfectly focused in their lower belly area. In aikido, kung fu, tai chi and chi gung, the energetic foundation stone is that your *chi* – your vital energy – is located in your belly. All movements in oriental martial arts centre round the lower belly.

Imagine a martial artist: feet apart, knees slightly bent, back straight, eyes calm and alert, breathing gently, energy carefully contained. Anything physical or energetic can happen around this person, and they will nevertheless remain calm and watchful. This is the precise poise that we all need to deal with atmospheric situations that cause us some difficulty.

Many years ago, while studying to go to university as a mature student, I ran a very tough bar in Somerset. One quiet Saturday lunchtime two 15-year-old girls, obviously under age, asked for alcoholic drinks. I refused them. They insisted and I refused them again. I then found myself confronted by a very large threatening man leaning over the bar into my face. He said they were his cousins and I had to serve them. His expression and tone were aggressively insistent. I myself am not a physical fighter, but I replied that I could not serve them. He insisted again.

I stayed calm and assessed the situation. I thought that I had a chance of calming him down if I could just get him into conversation. My main argument – man-to-man – would be that if I served them I would lose my job. Did he really want that? I knew, though, that I would need to have this conversation with him in private, because it would be difficult for him to back down in public.

Staying calm I asked whether he would come into a back room where we could discuss the subject privately. He looked at me long and very cold, perhaps for 15 seconds. He then half smiled, said it was not worth it and told his cousins to buzz off.

A week later, he and I were the only people in the bar, and we started drinking and chatting together. In fact, we got on well and I asked him about that first encounter. He laughed and then began to explain. He had, he told me, been fighting ever since he was a kid. He was from a gypsy family and had had to stand up for himself or be persecuted. But he also enjoyed fighting and I later learned he was considered the hard man of the area. As a fighter, he had studied his opponents' styles and in particular he always watched the body language of people as they began to prepare to fight. He explained that there was a spiral of threats that finally built up to an actual blow.

My body language that lunchtime, however, had not fitted the general pattern of the spiral towards violence. Nor, he noticed, was it the body language of fear. My breathing and facial expression were calm. My eyes were aware and steady. I showed no anxiety. I was physically comfortable. He, therefore, concluded that I was possibly a very sophisticated black belt karate expert who was inviting him into the back room to finish him off quickly and discreetly.

This is a very significant piece of information for people who want to lead dignified lives in a threatening world. The body language of calm awareness is the same body language of the most accomplished and confident fighter.

Again, if you look at the body language and the body energy of any effective martial artist, you will see that their physical body is calm and grounded, and the breath is gently even. Even when surrounded by a dozen threatening enemies, the body energy is kept calm, the eyes are observant.

I know that this may all sound very manly and macho, but it is an unavoidable reality that you must follow when you feel psychologically or energetically attacked, or when you are in an intense situation. The logic is infallible: if you want to feel calm and confident when attacked, then your actual physical body must feel calm and confident.

If you are fully in your body, calmly breathing and well

earthed, it is also easier to assess the situation and to assess possible strategies. If you are panicking, there is no psychological space to work out what to do.

I have heard many stories of how people have avoided being hurt by maintaining their energetic poise. One friend, walking late at night, saw a group of youths coming towards him on the other side of the street. He immediately sensed danger, started to freeze, but came back to his breath. One of the kids broke away from the group, came up to my friend and held a knife at his throat. My friend stayed calm and breathing while the world around froze for a minute, and then the boy walked on having done nothing. Sure enough my friend's fear surfaced several minutes later in shaking and severe distress, but he had maintained dignity and calm during the actual scene. Who knows what might have happened otherwise?

This is especially a crucial issue for women who, simply because they are women, face an ongoing threat from dysfunctional aggressive men. I need to be very clear about this because I do not want a single woman hurt because of advice that I give. I know from experience that this grounding energy work is the cornerstone of personal safety. But if you are dealing with highly charged aggressive men then you must have other strategies as well. One woman I know, when confronted once by three young men in a London underground station, took a long cool look at them and then went berserk. She attacked them with all her anger and frenzy, and they ran. She had no training in self-defence, but she was physically strong, and decided to fight and take the risks rather than go down passively.

In another situation her decision might well have been wrong, but that was the kind of character she was. In Chapter 6 of this book I describe some energy exercises for building up self-confidence and personal strength. These can also help you build up a 'front' that will put people off, but I also recommend to anyone who is nervous about being victimised that you are very practical and get some realistic training in self-defence and conflict resolution.

Remaining calm and centred, however, is the foundation.

Fear of your own fear

We also need to be calm and centred to feel atmospheres accurately. This is because the whole of the physical body is sensitive to what is in our auras. Usually, when we are frightened, certain parts of our body freeze and other parts of our psyche try to escape; in this kind of a state it is obviously impossible to be accurately sensitive. In fact – and here is a terrible irony – if we are frightened then the most powerful energy we are going to register is our own fear. I remember a startling experience of this happening to me when I was a teenager. I was staying in the countryside and had got lost coming home. A bat flew low and caught in my hair for a few seconds before releasing itself. I shuddered with fear. Although the bat had flown on I was then spooked by every possible shadow and movement which I felt electrocuting me through my aura – when I was in fact purely circulating my own terror. Luckily there are very easy techniques for achieving a calm and earthed body.

Special Note on How to Do the Exercises

All through the book you will be using exercises that require you to use your imagination or visualisation skills. It is important that you understand how to do this properly.

First, you need to feel calm and have a patient attitude. Second, do not expect dramatic perceptions and feelings. A lot of this work is very subtle.

When I ask you to imagine or sense something I want you to get a picture in your mind of it happening. At the same time I want you to have a subtle sense of feeling it in your body.

A very small number of people, when they do work like this, get very bright and clear pictures. But most people do not. I, for example, do not get clear movie images. The most important thing is to have a subtle sense of it happening. This simply requires an open and flowing mind.

So if, for example, I ask you to imagine or sense an energy running down your spine into the earth, I want you to close your eyes – do it with your eyes open if you can – and sense/feel/imagine/visualise this energy moving down through you. Just having the thought of it is enough. Trust that the process works. You will be able to experience the results. Do not worry if it feels very subtle and light. When I do the exercises myself I do not work with imagery very much, but more with a subtle sense or feeling of it. Also, do not worry if you feel clumsy doing the exercises. A little bit of practice will help you feel comfortable with them.

All the exercises in this book are based in the idea that *energy follows thought*. When you think of something, when you give something your attention, then energy flows in the direction of your focus. You can therefore use your mind and imagination to create specific energy movements and atmospheres. In this chapter, for example, many of the exercises use your mind and imagination to connect your physical body properly with the earth. In the next chapter your mind and imagination are used to build up a sense of protection and a force field that shield you. By thinking of a protective bubble and sensing it, the gentle force of your psyche actually directs and moulds energy into the right shape. One of the remarkable capacities of a human being is the ability to do this energy work.

But please remember it can all feel very subtle and do not expect bright colourful images or thundering experiences. This is not the way the inner world is sensed by human beings. If it were there would be no argument or scepticism about its existence! So do all the exercises in a relaxed way and enjoy the gentle flow that you feel when doing them.

Earthing

The basic feature of all earthing or grounding exercises – both phrases mean the same – is to get a sense of the energy of your body connecting deep into the energies of the earth itself. None of these exercises are complicated and they can be done quite casually, even for a few seconds while reading this book. Use whichever ones work for you and feel effective.

Focus your mind on the earth beneath you. Get a gentle sense of your connection with it. If you are several floors up, imagine the connection going down through all the floors below you. Feel this connection going ever deeper into the earth. Some people will feel the connection very easily. For others it is more subtle, so do not worry if it is not obvious to you. Over time it will build up.

There are many different ways you can help yourself to sense the connection.

Sense this connection with the earth down through the soles of your feet and down through the base of

29

your spine. If you have good visualisation skills, use those. Otherwise build up a gentle feeling of the energy running down through you into the ground.

You can sense the energy running all the way from the top of your head down through the length of your spine and body, down into the earth.

If there is a particular part of your body that experiences tension and anxiety, sense a link between that specific area and the earth.

Sense the energy going from the base of the spine down to the centre of the earth and then *looping back up* to the spine.

In oriental medicine there is an energy map of the body which includes certain specific centres known as chakras. It is good to anchor all the chakras, one by one, down into the earth: base of spine; sexual centre; solar plexus; heart; throat; forehead; crown.

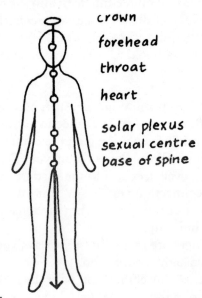

crown
forehead
throat
heart
solar plexus
sexual centre
base of spine

Earth every chakra

Imagine that you are a tree. Your torso is the trunk. You have deep descending roots.

Go out regularly and actually touch the earth with your bare feet or hands.

Hug trees and feel how deeply rooted they are. Sense the energy of trees going deep into the earth.

When walking along the street imagine that you are partly or completely under the ground.

Imagine that you are like a mountain.

Massage the soles of your feet with soil or with a powdered metal such as magnesium or aluminium.

Try wearing an amulet made of lead or haematite.

All these techniques build up their effectiveness when practised regularly. If you are particularly heady or intuitive, it is important to anchor the energy around your head, especially the crown, deep into the earth. I practise earthing myself from the time I wake up in the morning. In fact, remaining earthed as I move through a busy life in a large city is an ongoing and central part of my physical and psychological health. It is something at which I work continuously.

Being in the body

As well as being connected to the earth we have to be fully in our physical bodies. Modern civilisation, with all its stimulation, concrete and electricity, makes it very easy to forget about the physical body, and to live purely in a world that is psychological and cultural.

The most important exercise I know for being in your body is to hold a very gentle physical awareness as soon as you wake up every morning. It takes only a couple of minutes and is very pleasant. As you wake up, gently be aware that you have a body and that after a night's sleep you are bringing your consciousness back into your vehicle. As you wake up, do not start thinking about what you have to do that day or other pieces of personal business. Do not start worrying. Do not start rushing. Do not get out of bed immediately.

Spend some quiet time bringing your waking awareness fully into your body. Notice your toes and feet. Move them a little. Greet them. Bring your focus slowly all the way through your body. Do you have any particular aches and pains? Notice these aches and do not push them away. Greet them and take your consciousness warmly into them. Perhaps touch yourself where there is tension.

All of this shows your biological creature, your vehicle, that you are fully aware of it and this is physically reassuring. It is the first step towards being confidently and comfortably in your body. This exercise can work even if you are in physical pain; in fact it may bring some comfort.

It is also a very private exercise and even if you are sleeping with someone else, they do not need to know or suspect that you are doing it. Sometimes people fall back asleep having done the exercise. This is fine because the sleep should now be very relaxing. It is important, though, to wake up slowly again and be fully in your body before bounding off into your daily life.

There is another simple exercise which really helps. Sitting or lying comfortably, spend a while simply sensing particular areas of your body. What does it feel like in one of your calves or an ankle? With a little gentle concentration you should be able to feel your pulse in any area that you place your focus. This will bring your awareness into your whole body.

Here are a few other ways of bringing you into your body.

- Massage yourself.
- Receive massage.
- Enjoy a lazy bath.
- Regular physical exercise.
- Yoga.
- Dance and movement.
- *Do anything that makes you feel your body.*

If you have real trouble getting grounded and into your body, try a course in martial arts, tai-chi or chi gung. Even a short course will help you rebalance your centre of gravity and change your body awareness.

There is always someone who asks whether you can earth yourself while flying in an aeroplane and the answer is 'yes'. In fact earthing helps to relieve anxiety about flying. Just imagine a thread going down from you in the sky to the centre of the earth.

And there is always someone else who asks whether it is dangerous to ground yourself in a plane because it might pull the plane down to crash. To this I can only reply, not in my experience.

Breathing

At the same time that you ground and feel comfortable in your body, your breathing must be calm and rhythmic. It is obvious, isn't it, that a basic sign of calm self-control is a gentle rhythmic breath. If we are nervous, one of the first symptoms is that our breath becomes tight, irregular and shallow.

Normally, when everything is going smoothly, we do not notice – and we do not have to notice – the state of our breath. When, however, we are in an intense or threatening situation, or working with energies, we must notice whether our breath needs guiding out of tension into a comfortable rhythm.

This is a silent breath with no noise and no effort. The in-breath and the out-breath are of the same comfortable length. Traditionally people count to seven on their in-breath and seven on their out-breath, but you need only do this if you find it helpful. Many people can flow into a relaxed rhythm without counting.

You also have a choice between pausing for a second between each in-breath and out-breath, or letting the in-breath and out-breath slide gently into each other. It is worth experimenting with both. Try them both out and see which is easiest for you.

You do not have to worry or think about your breath if it feels comfortable, but you must learn the skill, when stressed, of guiding your breath into a gentle rhythm. If your breath is under control, then you yourself will feel under control. It is an essential skill that you must master if you want to feel free and confident.

Imagine, for example, that you are dealing with someone who is screaming abuse at you or trying to upset you. You just stand there, gently holding your focus and keeping a calm breath. You will feel good and you will be able to act creatively.

The perfect times to practise guiding your breath are when you have nothing better to do, for instance when travelling to work, or at an endless meeting, or in a queue that might otherwise drive you mad.

This is what to do.

Gently guide your breath so that it is regular and has a calm rhythm.

Guide it so that the in-breath and out-breath are of similar length.

Either have your exhalations and inhalations flowing

smoothly into each other, or have a small pause
between them. Use what feels easiest.
    Do not worry where the breath sits in your chest, for
it will find its appropriate location. You may, however,
if you are feeling particularly tense, want to take one
or two deep breaths to ease up your chest.

If, after much practice, you still find it very difficult to
guide your breath, try a course in yoga or meditation
where there is a focus on breath. If you can feel an
unmovable knot in your chest you may benefit from a
therapy called rebirthing which is a breathing technique
that dissolves deep tensions in the body. Deep tissue
massage may also help loosen up strangulated breath.
Many people also find voice exercises very useful.

Our geographical location

There is one other factor which can really support you in
feeling grounded and physically comfortable. This factor is
knowing where you are located on the physical earth. This
moment in time, as you read this book, I challenge you to
pause for a moment.
    Do you know where north, east, west and south are? Do
you know in which direction the nearest river is? Do you
know which way to turn to face the nearest ocean or to
watch the setting sun? Are you on a hill or a plateau? What
kind of earth is beneath you, clay, granite . . .?
    Let me pose a few more questions to you. Can you point
in the direction of your office or home? Can you point
towards your favourite mountain or river or lake? In which
directions are your loved ones and best friends?
    What has all this to do with energy work? Part of being

a natural biological creature on this planet is to know where you physically are. I am certain that, at a subconscious level, you need to know where you are in order to feel safe. Have you ever experienced getting lost in a forest or the countryside, or even in the city and suddenly going into panic? That panic is a vital piece of evidence concerning our natural instincts.

In rural and tribal societies people know naturally where everything is. Tribal people have to know where they are in order to survive. People who live in close relationship with the land would think it completely crazy not to know where they are. We are nature's creatures on this earth and, in order to feel secure, we need to know where we are located. It is as simple as that.

I therefore suggest that you get clear about where the four directions are in your homes and work places. East, just to remind you, is where the sun rises. If necessary get yourself a compass.

When you have marked in your mind the four directions, then sit quietly in your home or work place, and notice in which directions your favourite people and places are.

Very often when I want comfort or need a greater sense of safety, I orient myself to the four directions and think of my favourite places. I do this in quite an extravagant way. When I think of the west, I let my mind go all the way across the Atlantic to the Grand Canyon which is one of the most stunning and powerful places on earth. I go north to a place in Scotland where there are some wonderful ancient stones called the Clava Cairns in a beautiful valley. I go east to the Alps, to a mountain I love called Engelberg (Angel Mountain). And I go south to the High Atlas Mountains of Southern Morocco where I lived for two years.

At the same time that I connect with these places I also remind myself that I am on earth and make sure I am grounded. I also connect with the vast wilderness of sky above me. I could not survive happily in the city if I was not aware of these connections.

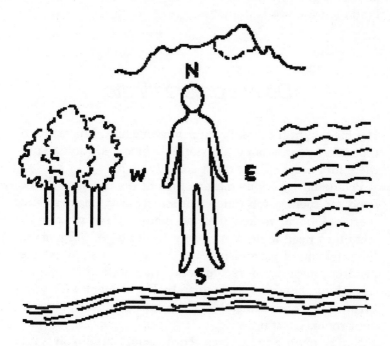

Know where you are physically located

Whenever you move house or work, spend time becoming familiar with the landscape of your new area. Look to see where the hills are and what the ground feels like under the buildings. Check for the nearest river and water. Go to the local library and get out old maps showing what the land was like before the concrete and tarmac was laid. Get a real feeling for the land on which you are living.

Imagine that you are in a really difficult meeting at work which is going on late and is full of tension. For a few moments you monitor your breath and grounding. You then orient yourself to the compass points, and to the places and beings you love. The natural support from this kind of awareness is immense.

Do not procrastinate

Having taught these skills for some time now, I have found that many people can understand them and are able to put them into practice, but don't actually do it.

People have various reasons for not doing what will be good for them – too much caution, anxiety, laziness and inertia. I have worked with so many people who know what they need to do, but simply do not do it. Forgive me then if I sound patronising, but I know that some people need encouraging. I recommend, therefore, that you do something, anything, immediately. Experiment with your breath. Try grounding. Mark the four compass points in your room. Do it now.

Some people may lack confidence. Again let me encourage you. This work is easy. There is a wonderful saying that ships are not built to stay in safe harbours. They are built for the open seas. So if you have an instinct for this kind of work, then don't be put off, get on with it. Your strength and courage are needed. Remember that this energy work can create a better and safer space for everyone.

To remind you, here is a summary of what you have learned in this chapter:

- Be grounded.
- Be calmly in your body.

- Gently breathe.
- Be aware of your geographical location.
- Be carefully discriminating.
- Do it.

3

Protection

Stay healthy

Feeling psychically vulnerable to external vibrations happens to most of us at some time or another. Most of us feel more vulnerable when we are stressed, or tired, or going through intense personal change. We become more sensitive to any kind of pressure and we cannot stand having people in our faces. We want even loved ones to keep their distance. If we become really vulnerable, we can sense people's moods too easily and this can be overwhelming. Situations where there are a lot of people in particular can become very difficult. Going to work wears us down and we begin, at worst, to burn out.

To be very practical, the first step in psychic protection is to get some sleep, rest and relaxation. There is no point in wallpapering over the reality that sometimes we are exhausted wrecks and therefore psychically vulnerable. We need to be rested and physically well. If our physical nervous system is weak, then we are also psychically weak.

Essentially, I am just reminding you of something very obvious, which is that you need to look after yourself. There is physical health and there is also psychic health, and they are interlinked. Remember that your sensitivity to atmospheres and energies anchors down through your nervous system. If your nervous system is physically exhausted, then you can be easily overwhelmed by changes in your energy field which would normally cause no tension or difficulty at all.

The first strategy then in psychic protection is to be healthy. Sleep. Get appropriate physical exercise. Eat good food. Stop drinking alcohol, smoking or using drugs. Manage your time better. Commit to less work. Rein in your ambition or workaholism. Use sensible strategies to live a decent and humane life.

I do not want anyone using the techniques of this book if it is to the cost of the more basic strategies of looking after yourself sensibly. I can imagine a dedicated reader struggling to earth, to breath calmly, to create psychic protection, to hold a clear awareness – when what they really ought to do is take the day off work or walk in the country or sit down next to a tree or sleep.

That said, there are definitely times when it is appropriate to be able to protect ourselves from external vibrations. Sometimes people are sceptical about this and say, 'Doesn't this mean that you are encouraging people to escape reality and to withdraw from relationships?' My reply to this is that life is not easy. There are times when we are overwhelmed or need some extra space. At these times we should be free to use strategies that will make life easier for us – and then we can deal more effectively with what is happening. When it is raining we wear raincoats; this does not mean that we are soft and avoiding reality. It is sensible and we take them off when it stops raining. Equally, we stop protecting ourselves energetically when our own inner climate changes.

In this chapter I present the basic protection techniques that you can use in all kinds of everyday situations. You may find them useful for just going into new situations or into the busy city; or you may want to use them when you know that you are going into a meeting where someone is actively hostile to you. I also describe how you can protect your home and how, if it is appropriate, you can protect someone else.

Bubbles of protection

The most well-known strategy of psychic protection is that of creating a protective bubble or egg around yourself. You imagine and sense yourself to be inside a bubble, and no unpleasant vibrations can penetrate it.

Get comfortable and relaxed.
   Earth yourself and guide your breath into a comfortable and relaxed rhythm.
   Imagine and sense that you are surrounded by a transparent protective bubble or egg, which protects you from negative vibrations.
   Spend a while sensing this bubble all around you. Over your head. Under your feet. Completely protecting your back. Completely surrounding you.
   Sense that your own vibrations can exit through the membrane of the bubble. Sense that the bubble does not prevent good energies from coming in.
   Be very relaxed and comfortable in it.
   Have a clear sense that unpleasant external energies cannot penetrate.

There are then certain refinements which you can add to your bubble. Feel free to experiment with them and discover which feel best, or which you can do most easily.

When you have made your bubble, exhale slowly and sense that your warm, moist breath carries your pure vibration – 'essence of you' – into the bubble. Fill your bubble with your own vibration. Do this for several breaths.

Fill the bubble with different colours. How does a green or blue bubble feel? Be psychedelic and try a rainbow-coloured bubble. At different times or in different situations, you may find certain colours work better for you. (Every colour, like every sound, has a different vibration. As your mood or the situation changes, so the different colour vibrations which suit you will change.) Keep experimenting over time with what works best for you.

Fill the bubble with protective images that you like. Often these will be religious symbols such as the cross, Star of David, five-pointed star or the Hindu symbol for AUM, which is considered to be the sacred sound of creation. They may be mythical images such as Hercules and Diana or images of religious figures whom you trust such as Jesus, Buddha or Kuan Yin. (I will explain later on about how and why these symbols are of genuine energetic help.)

Feel free to be your bubble's interior decorator and do anything you like within it that seems to help you and give it a stronger vibration.

Imagine particularly potent symbols – such as the cross or five-pointed star – on the outside of the bubble, thereby strengthening the membrane.

Write slogans on the exterior of your bubble, such as, 'Please keep out' or 'Bad vibrations blocked'.

Important reminder. Always be certain that the bubble goes under your feet and up your back. And, as always, be grounded and breathing.

The most frequently asked question about the bubble exercise is, how big should my bubble be? Most people find it best to work with one that extends for about 4 or 5 feet. Others make it bigger. I have known a few people whose bubbles are skin tight and they wear them like rubber gloves or diving suits. The bubbles are elastic so, if you are in a crowded situation, they do not burst or open but mould themselves around you instead of being penetrated.

The second most frequently asked question is, how long will the bubble last? This depends on how regularly you do the exercise, and on how much focus and energy you give to its creation. If, the next time you are in crisis, you try to create a bubble without having practised it before, your bubble will not be very effective. For it to work properly it needs some practice and repetition. A few minutes' practice every day for a couple of weeks should get you fully into the feel of it. Once you feel confident, you can create it when you need to.

If, for example, you are working as a schoolteacher and are on overload, then I suggest that you deliberately put some awareness into your bubble every hour or so.

If you suddenly find yourself in an intimidating situation and create a bubble on the spot, it will probably be effective for about 20 minutes before you need to give it some more focus. What you have to do is monitor how you are feeling and strengthen your protection whenever you feel it weakening because the outside atmosphere is getting through to you. You will definitely feel when it is working or when it is beginning to lose its potency.

The bubble exercise or any other form of protection will not make you cold and frigid to people, because inside your bubble you can have any attitude you like. Other people will not notice your bubble unless they are trying to intimidate you, in which case they will notice that they are having no effect. You may actually enjoy the experience of seeing someone try to wind you up.

Shields

This protection technique is found in many traditions all over the world.

> Imagine that you have some shields. These shields are usually circular and vary from being a few inches wide to being several feet in diameter. You then place your shield over whichever part of your body you feel is most vulnerable. My wife, for example, when dealing with people who are emotionally unstable puts a small shield, decorated with an equal-armed cross in a circle, over her solar plexus. These shields can be decorated in any way you want. If you relate to the traditions of tribal and indigenous peoples, then decorate them in a tribal manner that you know.

People usually place their shields over that part of their body which feels most sensitive and often in accordance with the chakra system of Indian medicine. For example, if you feel that someone is sexually predatory, you might cover the chakra known as the sacral centre around your reproductive organs. If you are dealing with someone's spiky emotions, the shield might go over the solar plexus. If someone is thinking too intensely, then place the shield in front of your eyes and forehead. Other people may have one large shield protecting their whole torso.

Some people use a shield made of mirror glass and they sense this shield actively reflecting whatever atmosphere is coming at them.

Again, feel free to experiment. If you like the kind of work presented in this book, then you will find yourself enjoying the experimentation for many years. Try different shapes and sizes. Colour and fill your shield with images of protection to which you relate.

Flame

This technique is more dynamic and confident than the shield. It suits a good assertive mood.

> Imagine yourself to be a vibrant burning flame. The base of the flame is deep in the earth and your body is the core (like a candle-wick) of the fire. You are flaming bright and powerfully. Your dynamism and your glow simply do not allow bad vibrations to get through to you. Bad thoughts and feelings burn up and melt as they come into your radiance. Experiment with different colours. Taught classically, the flame is violet and golden.
>
> No one, unless clairvoyant, will actually see the colours, but people may notice a more confident atmosphere about you.

The cloak

> Envelop yourself in a wonderful magic cloak. This cloak may be simple or it may be multi-coloured. Feel its protection. Draw it all around you.

Close down like a flower

This technique is useful when you leave a situation in which you have been particularly open and now find yourself going into a less friendly environment. This situation can be as normal and daily as leaving home for work; or it can be after a massage; or coming back into an urban environment after a walk in the park or countryside.

> You simply sense yourself to be a flower with your stem going deep into the ground and your petals open. You then sense the petals gently closing in on you, like any flower does at night. A tulip is a perfect model for this exercise.

Some people who work with the chakra system imagine each chakra to be a flower and sense them one by one closing their petals.

Lead curtain

This is a technique which is very useful for people living together but who sometimes need to feel a sense of space around them. It can be particularly helpful if you share a double bed and feel that your own vibration, or your partner's, is interfering.

> Build up a sense of a curtain hanging between you and the other person. Make sure this curtain goes into the floor and up to the ceiling. Then begin to sense that it is made of lead. Breathe gently and, on the outbreath, feel the warmth and moisture of your breath helping to make the curtain more dense and real. Your own vibrations and your partner's will then bounce off it.

Power animal

Some people feel mystically connected to certain animals. They feel and experience the spirit of the animal as an ally who helps them through challenging times.

If you have such a connection with an animal, you might like to try sensing that you are wearing a great magical head-dress and costume, made from the skin of the animal, and which makes you feel as if you actually are the animal. This ceremonial costume has an aura of power and protection.

Only try this technique if you have a clear sense of such an animal ally. Also, when you sense yourself wearing the skin, you need to feel completely mellow and comfortable within it, not excited or aggressive, not running any adrenalin. I repeat my nag: you are earthed, calm and breathing gently.

Power plants

Some people have a similar relationship with plants, especially large trees.

Again, feel yourself dressed as the tree, becoming the tree. Deep roots, strong trunk, radiant with natural energy, nothing unpleasant touching you.

Asking for help

Whatever protective technique you use, it can be made much more effective if you also plug into a major energy field of loving and beneficent energy. This is easier to do if you have a religious background or experience. You can then call upon the power of God or a great religious figure to help you. There will be more on that in Chapters 5 and 6.

Protecting your home

The basic bubble technique can also be used to create a protective membrane around your home.

> Sit quiet, grounded and breathing. Slowly begin to sense that your home is in a bubble of protection. Breathe your own energy into it. Sense the bubble not allowing in any disturbing vibrations. Colour the bubble. Decorate it. Experiment with what feels good. Try using the flame technique, or power animals and plants.
>
> If there are symbols that you like, sense them over or on your doors and windows. You can also use real objects to enhance the protection.

Feel free to use your instinct and intuition. My own back door, for instance, is guarded by a Green Man mask and the front door has three horseshoes over it. The front entrance also has a rosemary bush growing close to it which is a plant recognised for its purifying and protective essence.

The house is also protected by a more general aura that has been created over years of living in it. We light a candle every day and dedicate it to bringing harmony and peace into the home. Something similar to this is done in millions of households the world over. A small thought and prayer every day over years builds up a natural dynamic of protection which permeates the physical structure and aura of the home.

When we go away, we leave more powerful protection. My wife Sabrina and I discovered that we both did this early on in our marriage. We were going on holiday and a mile from home, Sabrina asked whether I had put up any special protection around the house. I have known a few thieves and know that when they do a burglary, they are very cautious and always on edge, looking for any sign that might get them into trouble. Their energy bodies are poised to pick up threatening signals and they are sensitive to atmospheres. So I had created a specific defence to unnerve them. I had created in thought energy, at the back and front doors, and at vulnerable windows, the image and feeling of a helmeted London policeman, truncheon raised in one hand, saying, 'You're arrested!'

Sabrina laughed and I then asked her whether she had put up special protection. She nodded and said that the house was surrounded by an ocean filled with huge, hungry, angry sharks who hated burglars.

We haven't been burgled. (We also lock the doors and windows!)

Protection through loving

There is another strategy for protection which uses a completely different approach. This particular technique also carries very interesting psychological benefits.

Again, its essence is not complicated. If an energy or atmosphere is coming at you, then it is possible to send an opposing energy directly at it to bounce it away.

If someone sends a negative thought at you, then it is possible to push it away with an equally powered negative thought of your own. But this creates further problems because you will have then produced more negative energy which pollutes the general psychic environment. This is not ethically sound. It will affect other people. Also, more personally, the echo of your action will attract something similar back to you.

Instead of reacting with a similar negativity, a more creative strategy is to respond with love – to respond with a positive and generous bolt of energy. Let's be very practical about this. If you send love to an energy that is attacking you, then the energy of your love will actually block and push away the attack. Love is a positive and creative force which, when expressed dynamically, repels negativity.

You might say that it is hypocritical to send love if you do not, in fact, love your attacker. I respond that what is called hypocrisy here is a step towards an attitude of forgiveness. I am not talking about a passive or stupid love in which we lie down like a dog waiting to have our stomachs scratched. I am describing mature and empowered human beings who have decided that they have had enough of unhealthy attitudes and negative vibrations. They just want to get on with a decent life and this means having certain positive attitudes.

Loving your enemy is also psychologically helpful because it cuts through patterns of victimisation and aggression. It means coming to a centre of confidence and goodwill. It means aligning with good, with beauty and with love. It does not mean approving of actions that are intolerable. It means setting up an opposing energy field that is powerfully benevolent.

There are two different ways of doing this.

1. Electric love your enemy

This is a Buddhist practice for loving your enemy that I was taught many years ago. It is very powerful and effective for holding off a negative energy field, and can be used when you feel as if you are under some kind of energetic attack.

There is a special hand position that goes with this exercise (see illustration). It is not necessary to use it, but the body language can help take you into the right mood. Place your right thumb against your heart with your fingers pointing up. Place your left thumb, fingers still pointing up, alongside the little finger of your right hand. Be calm and grounded.

Get a sense of your 'enemy'. Without hesitation or any holding back, send a laser beam of goodwill and love from your heart and head directly at him or her. At the same time, with absolutely clear intent, mentally repeat quickly over and over again 'I love you, I love you, I love you'. This love shoots with amazing electric force from you into and around the person.

Do this for at least a minute or even as long as five minutes. Repeat the exercise as often as you feel appropriate. Just reading about it, you can imagine, I hope, the power of this technique.

I have known people in my classes, however, who get themselves into a mental knot with this exercise, saying that they simply cannot bring themselves to love their opponent. They are blocked from even beginning to do it. This occurs particularly with people who have experienced genuine abuse. There are various techniques that can help cut through this resistance. For example, imagine that you are an actor and you have to act the part with total authenticity, as in method acting. Simply act it as if it were true and do the exercise as an experiment in theatre. Then see what it feels like.

Alternatively you can think of your enemy in a way that helps you view them in a different light. Imagine them as

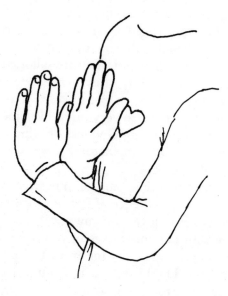

'I love my enemy.'

a child or a little baby. Look into their heart and soul, and see their true self struggling to be present. Imagine them lying vulnerably curled up in bed. Imagine them naked. Use anything that will reframe your attitude so that you can perceive them as a weak and vulnerable human being, rather than as a totally negative oppressor.

2. Calling on the goddess

There is a second way of loving your opponent in which the style is much more female. It still requires complete clarity of intention and a confidence that we feel through our bodies.

In this technique, go quiet and centred, and begin to tune into the vast love and beauty of the universe. The universe can be experienced as an ocean of warm love. Sometimes when people talk about a female deity, about goddess rather than god, they are talking about this experience of the totality of existence being a warm energy field of affection and nurture. This way of experiencing Spirit is also very juicy, like ripe fruit, and like Kali, the destroying Goddess of Hinduism, is very understanding about the natural processes of birth, death and rebirth.

With absolute authenticity and calm passion, you tune into this great experience of female deity, this cosmic ocean of warm love, and you ask it to embrace, hold and love your opponent. Again, you repeat this prayer with complete sincerity for at least a minute and up to five minutes. Do this as often as you feel is appropriate. The words of a prayer could be something like this: 'Goddess of all creation. Great ocean of love and nurture. Mother who brings all things into life, hold and embrace my oppressor with all your love and power. Help this person to surrender to your love and the love of the cosmos.' For it to work, however, you have to feel the loving power yourself.

Protecting someone else

I am often asked whether it is possible to protect someone else, especially a loved one or child. This can be a problem because it is debatable whether we have the right to protect other people from their own experiences. In Chapter 7 I devote some attention to the ethics and rules of using these techniques for other people.

It is in the very nature of a caring relationship, however, to want to guard friends, relatives and lovers from distress. Whether it is right for you to do this for someone else cannot be judged mentally. In the depth of your heart, from a feeling of detached wisdom, you will know whether it is appropriate to try and protect another person. And if you do decide to help someone, then you have to make absolutely certain that your own attitude is 100 per cent pure and centred. If you are in any way anxious, over-protective or worried about the other person, then your vibration of anxiety will be transferred across to the other person, perhaps only making things worse.

If you can be fully centred and calm, then you can very gently use all the techniques listed above and transfer them across to support someone else. If you feel the slightest personality desire or worry then do not even begin to do it. In general I would also say that you should never do it for another adult unless you have their permission.

In other words, if in doubt, do not do it. If you are certain that it is appropriate and that you are not over-protective or interfering, then gently go ahead. When working on behalf of someone else, you absolutely must be grounded, in the body, breathing gently and centred. This way you can be certain that your vibration is beneficent.

The best form of protection, though, is to teach these basic techniques, for example, to your own family. And here is a home truth that you may find uncomfortable: the best way to teach these things to close relatives, especially your own children, is to set an example and model the behaviour yourself. If your own children are half out of their bodies and nervy, then it is probable that you are too. So do not try and teach these things to other people – or help them energetically – until you have first mastered them yourself.

Coming from the countryside into the city

If you live in the country you may well have uncomfortable problems when you come into the city. Some people are simply overwhelmed by it. I remember well how shaky I was in the city after returning from my two-year retreat in the mountains without electricity or running water. The stimulation was very uncomfortable and it took me three months to stabilise.

It was in response to that crisis that I learned what is needed to be able to deal with the urban atmosphere. I am also certain that a lot of the problem lies not so much in the city vibrations, but in our being cut off from the vibrations of landscape and nature.

There is a very easy and effective exercise for solving all this. It is similar to the strategy of knowing where you are geographically located which I described in the last chapter. It is an exercise that needs doing once a day for several, say four, weeks before it becomes fully effective. Basically it connects you with nature and wilderness wherever you are.

Get grounded and centred. Then let your awareness wander off towards the north, east, south and west. (The order does not matter.) In each case let your mind stretch until it finds an area of unhindered nature or wilderness. You could, for example, go west to the Atlantic Ocean, north to the Arctic, east to the Siberian Steppes, south to the Sahara Desert.

Then let your mind go down deep into the earth and then high up into the sky.

Recognise that you are at the centre of a six-armed star. State clearly to yourself, either aloud or only in your mind: 'Wherever I am, I am energetically connected with the wilderness of the earth below me, the heavens above me, and the landscape far beyond me.' Feel the connections.

Then, when you come into the city, feel exactly the same connections. Feel them through the concrete and past the built-up areas. It is easy to maintain the connections. We do not have to lose these connections simply because we are in the city. If we maintain these connections in the urban milieu, then our bodies – our energy bodies – will feel secure and nurtured, even though we are in the urban electricity.

I deliberately work on these connections at least once a day. When you are overworked or feeling particularly stressed, you may need to reconnect with wilderness several times a day. During these stressful periods make a point of going to the park or outside as often as you can. You will find it well worth getting up earlier so that you can have some peaceful time with nature. Make a point of noticing the nature around you, including the flowers and potted plants. Touch and hug trees. Touch the earth.

It is easy to remember to do these things when we are feeling well. It is even more important to do them when the pressure is on.

I know several people who have bought compasses in order to know how they are aligned wherever they are and I know others who put them on the dashboards or windscreens of their cars. One inner city nurse, whose work is mainly house visits, has turned her whole car into a little sanctuary with a compass and small photographs of her favourite places in the landscape. Between patients, she always takes a few minutes' quiet time, aligning with the four directions and using the images to help connect her. She is a good example of how this kind of inner work can be of effective use to someone who lives permanently in the city.

Knowing the enemies within

It is important to have some understanding of the energies within our own aura. We are often attacked by our own inner shadows, repressed parts of the psyche, and we then blame other people. When we encounter an atmosphere we do not like, there is always the possibility that its source is in our own psyche and aura. This needs to be explained carefully as it is one of the greatest pitfalls of inner work.

Psychologically we have all been wounded in one way or another in the past. These wounds are often repressed so that we no longer remember them, but they sit in the unconscious mind and emotions. These repressed parts are not just in the mind-brain, but are bubbles of energy which we hold in our aura without recognising them.

Imagine perhaps that you were victimised by someone when you were young, but you never had the opportunity to weep or retaliate or heal. The experience of victimisation would then sit within you as a pocket of unresolved energy. It may contain fear, anger, resentment and so on. It is there, but not conscious.

Then one day you may find yourself in a situation which brings this energy in you to the surface. You do not know that it belongs to you, so it is natural to blame something outside yourself.

The experience of your own shadow energy may be triggered by various events. Perhaps you meet someone else with a psychological pattern and history very similar to your own. They too were victimised and never healed it. The vibration of their own repressed wound will connect with the vibration of your own repression, triggering it. We need to understand that we carry all kinds of unconscious patterns and defence mechanisms which sit as energies in our aura; and they are liable to be triggered by anyone with the same history. There is a famous new age truism that is used when you do not like someone: What unintegrated aspect of yourself does that person represent?

Or you may find yourself meeting someone who reminds you of your abuser and that is enough again for your own psychological process to throw up your repressed energy.

There are also very powerful landscapes where the natural swirling energy of the earth shakes up repressed energetic material. I have met several people, for instance, who swear that Glastonbury Tor in south-west England is a negative power point because of the bad experiences they had there. The Tor is indeed powerful, but in a neutral way and its natural vortex of energy was only releasing stuff in them that was finally ready to surface.

It is obvious, therefore, that we have to be very careful when using any psychic protection. Instead of defending ourselves from something out there, we may in fact be repressing something inside. Psychic protection is very useful for providing space to deal with a difficult situation; but we must not ignore or further repress the wounds that need healing.

For years I used to say in my workshops that I was a naturally sensitive type and that I was not used to pubs or bars, so I needed to put myself in a protective bubble before entering them. I said this for years and I believed it, and my groups believed it. One day, however, I was listening to myself teaching and I realised that it was not true.

The reality was that I used to spend a fair amount of time in pubs, and I was rough and harsh as a teenager and in my twenties. Years later my harshness had not disappeared completely, but was happily repressed, sitting unconsciously in my aura. When I went into a pub, therefore, the rough vibrations of the place were triggering my own unintegrated violence. In fact, I was feeling my own repressed violence – not the violence of the place.

I have also counselled several people who thought that

they were being energetically attacked by unpleasant outsiders, but in fact were meeting unrecognised aspects of themselves. One young woman felt that there was a completely separate presence in her room who was haunting her. She even had conversations with this attacker. Working together it unfolded that this was such a powerfully repressed aspect of herself that it had almost taken on a life of its own. Over a few sessions she began to talk with it, make friends with it and gradually understand that it was indeed part of her. Over a few months, this aspect of herself was integrated and she was able to live her life without this constant sense of being attacked.

In all of this inner work, therefore, it is important to keep our scepticism switched on. We may never be 100 per cent accurate in our perceptions and insights, but we can have 100 per cent integrity if we are always open to being wrong. I work with the image of two radar dishes growing out of my head, scanning inside and outside for bullshit. Keep your bullshit scanners switched on.

At the very beginning of this chapter I reminded readers that the first strategy in psychic protection is to have a healthy body and nervous system. A healthy personality is also required. Of course, we all have our individual quirks and neuroses, but an ability – from a basis of strength and confidence – to laugh at ourselves and be generous to our enemies, is a good beginning for the psychological health needed to do this energy work.

4

Cleansing

Healthy energy moves

Healthy energy is energy that moves.

In the 1980s one of the smaller lakes on the United States and Canadian border was so polluted by industrial waste that it was considered a disaster which might take up to a hundred years to recover. Local legislation was passed to prevent further pollution and the water was allowed to flow in its own natural way. The lake came back to health within five years. This is possible with the polluted seas and lakes all over the Earth.

Stagnant water is a good example of how an energy whose natural state is movement creates a polluted environment if not allowed to flow. If it is simply allowed to move, it becomes and is healthy again. Students of Rudolph Steiner, the spiritual teacher who founded the system known as anthroposophy, have even produced a water cleansing system which has no filters of any kind but relies purely on moving the water through various spirals and vortices.

Anyone who lives in a city and has walked the streets at dawn will know the fantastic cleansing effect of the floods of fresh energy vitalised by the first rays of sunlight moving through the streets.

Students of energy have long known that one of the basic secrets of health is to keep energy and the body moving.

The most basic strategy of cleansing then is to get the energy moving. When we sense that something needs cleansing, we are usually aware of an atmosphere that is stuck in the fabric of that thing – a room, clothing, an object. All solid materials can hold an atmosphere because there is space within its atomic structure which can absorb a particular quality or vibration. To remove that vibration, we therefore need to do something that energetically goes into the fabric of the place, object or person to genuinely shift it.

So we can be quite logical about psychic cleansing if we focus on the essential principle: there is an atmosphere locked into some space which needs to be set into motion so that it moves on.

Some people worry that releasing atmospheres in this way pollutes the planet with negative energy. This is not so because, in nearly all cases, once the energy is moving, it becomes healthy simply because it is moving. I deal with a few cases of genuine negativity in Chapter 6.

Preparation

When you cleanse a space you have to be careful about the attitude with which you do it, because the quality of your attitude radiates into your work. Some people, for instance, hate housework or do it begrudgingly. They then complain about the atmosphere in their homes which they want to cleanse. What they do not realise is that, every time they clean, they radiate their unpleasant attitude and resentment into the very fabric of their homes.

This brings us back, once again, to this business of being calm and grounded. If you want a space to feel good, then when you do your cleansing work you must do it with a pleasant attitude, or else you just defeat the whole object.

> Before cleansing any space, therefore, bring yourself to a calm centre. Go into the room and sit quietly. Let yourself relax, ground and guide your breath into a comfortable rhythm. Then, when you are feeling calm, allow yourself to get a sense of the space. What does it feel like? Greet the space as if it were alive and had consciousness.
>
> Open your eyes and slowly look around. Notice the state of the floor, walls and ceiling. Take everything in.
>
> If you are cleansing a house and if you have the time, sit quietly in every room and go through the same procedure. If you do not have the time, then sit quietly in one room and then walk slowly around the whole house. Look in every nook and cranny. Open every cupboard and door. Look in the attic and under the stairs.

By doing all this, you take your awareness fully into the space where you, or someone else, work or live. It is a half-hour investment which can pay very comforting and supportive dividends. (If you have the time and opportunity, do it in rooms where you are about to have an important or difficult meeting.) By letting your consciousness travel slowly around the space, you ensure that you go ahead with the actual cleansing with the right attitude and vibration. Cleanse and decorate a space speedily, and your space will then contain a speedy atmosphere.

Physical cleaning

Having carefully familiarised yourself with the space, you can then get on with the process of deciding what actually needs doing. You need to be very practical. It is no use energetically cleansing a room which first needs a good clean or stripping. In some houses there are layers of wallpaper carrying decades of stuck atmosphere. The energy cleansing must be preceded by a thorough physical cleansing. It is no use complaining about a room which has layers of old carpet. Sometimes it is best even to strip the floors back to fresh wood.

Theoretically, it is of course possible to put a good vibration into a filthy tip. To do this, however, would take a year or so, and you would have to be one of the nicest, most relaxed and heart-centred saints in the world, so that your consistently wonderful vibration radiates into the atomic matter of the place.

But most of us do not want to live in a tip. We need the support of a clean environment.

Some people, however, have real trouble cleaning. When I say that the best physical cleansing is done with an attitude of enjoyment and love, they look sick. If this sounds like you, there is an imaginative exercise which can help.

In this exercise, you relax and close your eyes. Then think of the filthiest place in your home. This is usually the grease behind the fridge or cooker. Take your focus into the filthy grease, right into one of the carbon atoms that make up the old butter or margarine or whatever it is. The next phase is to focus on the fact that the one single atom in the grease is like a small solar system with glowing and moving energy particles. It is radiant and beautiful. It is easy to be impressed by the charm of the single atom, even to have some affection for it.

In this exercise the mind is seduced into loving the filth through focusing on a single atom. As the mind is brought back to look at the bigger picture, the grease is no longer a disgusting mess which you would do anything to avoid touching. It can be loved and cleaned with love.

It is also important, if you employ people to do cleaning, building or decorating, that they have a good attitude to their work. I once had friends decorating my house and found them playing heavy metal music and arguing in my bedroom. I had enough trouble in my relationships without having to deal with their vibration soaked into the walls of my bedroom. They understood and calmed down.

It is worth looking round to find friendly rather than resentful workers.

Use of vibration and aroma

The thorough physical cleaning of a place requires vibration to dislodge the atmospheres. Vibration is naturally created by sweeping, mopping, beating, wiping and vacuuming, all of which work directly into the fabric of the floors and walls. When doing this physical cleaning, keep the windows open so that air circulates and takes the dislodged atmosphere out into the wider world. Giving a room a 'good airing' is often what is precisely needed to cleanse it of a mood or feeling.

The physical cleaning can be helped by the deliberate creation of vibration. Stamping around the floor is good; so is hitting the floors and walls. Curtains, mattresses, cushions and soft seats particularly require a good thwacking. You may, for example, often teach or work in meeting rooms which are still thick with the atmosphere of the previous group. Chairs particularly hold the vibration of groups, especially padded chairs. If possible open all the windows, shake the chairs and thwack their seats. What is actually best is to take the chairs out into fresh air and shake or hit them outside.

I had one friend who often had overnight visitors and she was fastidious about cleansing the atmosphere of her guest room after each visitor. The windows would be opened, loud music with a strong bass vibrated through the room (Brahms or rock, depending on her mood), eiderdowns hung outside, and everything thumped with a tennis racket, including the mattress which would also be turned. She was still doing this ritual when she reached 80 and I can attest that staying in her guest room was always a fresh delight.

Sound can be used to create vibration in the air and fabric of any room or object. The bass notes at full blast on a church organ are a good example of vibration clearing a space. Similarly, Tibetan monks use 10-foot-long trumpets to create a cleansing vibration, along with clashing cymbals, bells and vibrant chanting. You should use the kind of sound that you like, but you need to be certain that it vibrates strongly enough to resonate through the room or object and actually move stuck energy. Sweet tunes and fairy bells do not. Drums and bagpipes are perfect. Play your stereo system at full volume for five minutes every few weeks and let the sound vibrate through your home. Any time that you feel the energy is stuck, bang a drum with a good bass resonance.

Some aromas also have a dynamic which is perfect for cleaning. (Different smells have different vibrations just as sounds do.) Some of these scents – such as mint, lavender and pine – are so well known for their cleansing properties that they are actually used in mass market products. In the East, the most frequently used cleansing scent is sandalwood. Native Americans burn sage, often sold in western shops as 'smudge sticks'. All these aromas have a dynamic and sharp vibration which dislodges stuck atmospheres.

Using scents, such as essential oils or incense, requires no ceremony. Just light them up and let the smell fill the room. You can have windows open from the beginning or just at the end. And you can, of course, use noise and scent at the same time.

Holy water can also be used very effectively to dislodge stuck atmospheres. In the next chapter I describe how to make holy water and the general principles of blessing which can be used all the way through the cleaning and cleansing process.

Salt

Salt has the startling property of being able to absorb depressed or 'heavy' vibrations in a room. We all know that if we leave salt out in the air, it absorbs moisture out of the atmosphere. It can also absorb generally negative vibrations. I do not know why or quite how it works, but it does. It is a general property of crystals to be able to absorb and hold atmospheres. This is also precisely why crystals were used in the original wirelesses and telephone receivers, because they catch the radio vibrations so easily.

Some people leave a bowl of salt regularly sitting in a room to absorb negative atmospheres, changing it every few days. Or they put it out after an argument or when difficult visitors have been in their home.

For a while I had a bowl of salt sitting outside our front

door when my son was spending time with a particularly tough gang of graffiti artists and skateboarders. He would come home with these grunting teenage hulks and, aware that we did not appreciate their vibration overwhelming the apartment, he would ask them to drain their energy off into the salt. Brought up on *Star Wars* and other magical realities, his posse of outlaws understood exactly what he meant, placed their palms over the bowl of salt and dutifully buzzed their energy into it. They thought it was cool.

Because crystals absorb atmospheres so easily they need special treatment if they are to be cleansed. There are several methods: leave them soaking in bowls of salt water for several days. Bury them in earth and allow the currents of the earth to draw out the atmospheres. Hold them in the ocean for a while and let the moving salt water absorb the vibration.

Stabilising the atmosphere

After an atmosphere has been disturbed, for example by a difficult business meeting or chaotic party, it is useful to stabilise and rebalance it. There is a wonderfully simple procedure which works very efficiently and easily. It involves placing an object representing one of the classical four elements – earth, water, air and fire – each in a corner of the space. It can be used to stabilise whole homes and buildings or just one room. You can do it regularly in your guest room after people have been staying; or in your bedroom if you have argued; or for the whole house if you have had a large, noisy group in it.

The procedure does not have to be exact or done with any ceremony. Just take an object which, for you, represents the element and place it approximately in one of the four corners of the space. If the space is L-shaped, for instance, just place the objects in the four corners and do not worry about the lack of square symmetry.

For earth, you could use a small cup of salt. You could also use rocks or crystals or soil.

For water, use a glass of water.

For air, use burning incense, the rising smoke representing air; or a feather, or a fan.

For fire, use a candle or oil lamp. Where it is impossible to use a naked flame, I know people who have used a piece of red satin or red aluminium foil.

Within minutes of placing the objects you will find the atmosphere beginning to settle. I have worked with many sceptics who could not believe that something like this would work, but I encourage them to try it and they are always surprised at how obvious the change in atmosphere is.

It is best to leave the objects sitting there for at least a couple of hours, perhaps even a few days. Do not worry about the incense burning out; you can leave it or light some more every few hours. When you clear the objects away, you can flush the salt and water down the drain or scatter them in the garden.

This particular system works with the four elements and corners. There is also an oriental tradition which uses five elements – earth, water, wood, fire and metal – and places specific objects in specific areas of your space. You will find details of this art of placement in any book on Feng Shui, which is the Chinese name for this harmonising energy work.

Cleansing yourself

Giving yourself a good shake has precisely the same effect as sending a vibration through a room. It releases energy that is blocked or glued into you. This, in fact, is as relevant to psychic protection as it is to cleansing, because people often feel energetically attacked or vampirised when, in fact, they are simply experiencing energy that is stuck and not moving. Moving and shaking your body will free up your own frozen energy, as well as moving any that belongs to someone or something else.

Let me give you a frequent example of stuck energy. You might meet someone whose attitude, for one reason or another, you find threatening or provocative. Because of the situation or because of the kind of person you are, you do not react visibly or directly towards your antagonist. Nevertheless you come out of the situation feeling terrible: tension in the stomach or solar plexus, muscle pain or headache, or a general sense of heaviness or weariness. You perhaps curse yourself for not remembering to have put up your protection. It's too late and you have been injured!

Or at least you think you have been injured. In fact, 90 times out of 100 you are only experiencing the pain of anxious energy that has frozen and locked into a part of your body. The quickest way to unload it is to move your body.

Shake. Stretch. Skip. Bounce. Move around. Do anything that gets the whole of your physique moving and shaking.

In terms of psychic health, protection and cleansing, people need to understand that they must regularly move their bodies. It is as much needed for psychic as physical health. If you do not move your body regularly then energy gets stuck, becomes stagnant and causes distress.

This one piece of information – that moving the physical

body loosens and releases stuck energy – can bring great relief. I have known dozens of people who, in discomfort, thought that they were dealing with some complex psychological and energetic problem, when all they had to do was shake. I genuinely mean *shake*. The next time you have an uncomfortable meeting, go somewhere where no one will mind and just give your body a good shake: hands, elbows, shoulders, head, torso, hips, legs and feet. Wobble your physical self. As you shake your head, feel your cheeks and tongue wobble. You may be very surprised by the release that it brings you.

You might also want to experiment with making interesting noises of release. Screaming, gasping and moaning are time-honoured techniques for shifting tension. When my partner leads workshops, she often experiences tension in the group that can be released with a good scream. She ask people who want to scream to identify themselves and then she and they disappear to make some ghastly high-pitched noises, later returning looking immensely serene.

There are some traditions which specifically teach the use of sound for cleansing and healing. The Hindu sound AUM can be sounded out with a focus on releasing psychic blockages. Spending a minute or so vibrating the AUM and then giving yourself a good shake can be a very effective ritual.

Running water can also be very helpful. It is fluid moving energy that cleans, washes and drains away psychic gunk that is stuck to our bodies. I often think of medical doctors and other therapists who wash their hands between patients. Certainly their hands need washing for physical hygiene, but the flowing water also helps wash away the energy of the previous patient. The pause between patients also allows the practitioner some space to calm, ground and come back to centre.

I have worked with hundreds of medical people, therapists and counsellors, and I think they are crazy not to take at least a minute's break between clients. In this minute they can practise some small ritual for their own personal psychic health and hygiene, even if it is just opening the windows and stretching. Ideally they ought to take several minutes, open the window, stretch, shake, walk, wash their hands and sit quietly for some seconds to centre and integrate their energies.

This kind of practice is relevant to anyone working intensely with people in any business, service or profession. It is crucial for anyone having many meetings with people to take some time out between sessions to 'clean up'. People who work in offices or are located in just one spot, should find an excuse to go walk-about every hour, not just to stretch your legs and back, but to keep your energy moving and your aura comfortably clean. It is a very simple form of self-care which can go a long way to preventing exhaustion and burn-out, and make you feel generally better. Some people I work with are really lazy and, at the very least, I say to them, get up regularly and look out of the window at the sky and clouds.

At home in the evening, if you feel clogged up with the energies of the day, get rid of them. Take off your working clothes, put them in the wash, or give them a good shake, or a good airing. Give yourself a stretch and shake, and then have a shower or bath; or let some fresh air roll over your body. Let the water or the air move the day's energies off you. If soaking in a bath, use some cleansing oil. Or burn some cleansing incense and waft the smoke over your body. Don't forget to release atmospheres stuck in your hair. Wash it and give your head a good shake.

Experiencing your own space

There is something else that is very important for personal cleansing which is to make sure that you do not have people in your energy field all the time. It is normal and healthy to need a sense of having your own personal space. With no one else in it, you can feel your own energies and quality without outside interference, and regain some personal equilibrium.

If you are living an intense people-filled life, for example as a parent or carer, you need to take regular spaces on your own. You may feel that this is impossible, but there are always moments through the day when you suddenly have an oasis of calm – in the bathroom, while everyone is watching television, washing up, pushing the pram in the park. These moments – even if only a minute or two long – can provide you with invaluable nurture and cleansing, providing that you also use the basic techniques of grounding, breathing and calming.

Years ago I was inspired by a single parent who saved herself from frantic craziness by walking her infant and pushchair very calmly and deliberately, feeling the earth beneath her, calming her breath and sensing her body. She deliberately walked near or under trees to feel their strength and rooting. Another woman I knew who had to entertain a lot, even though she felt easily overwhelmed, would regularly 'disappear' to wash some glasses, grounding herself by the sink and feeling the flowing water draining away into the earth. At intense meetings, I know successful business people who let their gaze move to the window and out into the great wilderness of the sky; for a minute they energetically ignore the meeting, create some space for themselves, and then refocus, energised and clear.

All these techniques of cleansing can be powerfully enhanced by using the energy techniques of blessing which are described in the next chapter.

5

Blessing

What is blessing?

It is best to start with a definition: 'A blessing is any transfer of energy which helps and encourages life to fulfil its potential.' I believe that every aspect of life has its own distinct essence whose purpose is to fulfil its potential. Everything is changing and growing in order to fulfil itself. To bless someone or something is to move energy through your own aura and then into the person, object or space so that it has a good and helpful effect. The basic energy with which we work in blessing is *unconditional love*.

To give a blessing is to deliberately go into the best possible, most loving mood of which you are capable, to connect with the energy field of unconditional love; and then to channel that love out into the atmosphere or into something specific.

This may sound ambitious, but everyone can do it. To one degree or another, for better and for worse, you are always unconsciously channelling some vibration into the atmosphere. To bless is to consciously radiate a beneficent vibration. In fact, when you are calm, relaxed and grounded, you naturally radiate a blessing. Many people notice a tangible atmosphere of calm peace when they enter a research library or place of worship where people are silent. Places of meditation and prayer can have fantastically beautiful atmospheres.

This ability to cleanse and transform the atmosphere of a space can also have very practical benefits. I have worked with several social workers who use these techniques precisely to help change the feeling in difficult and violent homes. I also know people who help to keep the general atmosphere of their workplaces clean and feeling good. I have known several bosses who do it, either for better productivity or to provide more pleasant working conditions for their workers. I have also known many people who do it just as an act of service for their colleagues. My wife, taking her driving test for the second time, cleaned up and blessed the dismal and anxiety-permeated waiting room, figuring that even if she failed she might as well do something useful for other people – and she passed.

The natural blessing of our core self

When we are calm and quiet, we produce a pleasant vibration. This is partly due to the calm radiation. But it is mainly due to the fact that being calm allows the energy of our core self to become present. Normally the activity of our mind and emotions is too jazzy and electric to allow the vibration of our core self to be felt.

The core self is a very important concept which you have to understand if the whole business of blessing is to make any sense. As we all know, our personalities change the vibration they radiate according to the kind of mood we are in. A bad mood radiates a bad vibration. A good mood vibrates a good vibration. But there is a core self, an inner self, in all of us which is always in a benevolent and understanding mood.

It is a universal experience that when people calm down their feelings and thoughts they begin to experience a new aspect of themselves. We certainly feel calm, but within the calm there is yet another sense of well-being. It is far deeper than just feeling relaxed. It is a well-being that is wise, accepting, tolerant, open and very benevolent. When we experience this feeling, we also experience who we really are inside all the psychological and social skins of our everyday personality.

Our core self has a distinctly pleasant energy field which it never losses. It is a subtle atmosphere so that we do not feel it when we are involved in our personality lives, but the moment we go quiet and relaxed we can begin to feel it. There are many religious arguments about what the core self – also called the soul, higher self, inner self, spirit, Christ within, atman, multi-dimensional self – really is: whether it reincarnates, whether it dissolves, whether it is a part of our biology, and so on. The only important thing to know in the context of this book is that the core self has a wonderful atmosphere and is naturally connected to the beneficent energies of the universe.

Go into any home where someone sits calmly and relaxed for a while every day, and you will always feel a serenity in the house. Some meditation teachers, in fact, have suggested that if there were just a few meditators in every neighbourhood, everything would change for the better.

Although the atmosphere of the core self is subtle, there are times when people have an overwhelming experience of their inner beauty. It happens at different times for different people, but suddenly they become overwhelmed by a sensation of beauty and bliss as they experience the energy of their own core. It may happen through meditation or prayer, or through dance or being in landscape, or through making love or nurturing an infant.

These can be overwhelming experiences of beauty. Most of the time, however, we need deliberately to relax our bodies and personalities, in order to feel the gentle impression of our inner self energy.

I believe that people should do whatever works for them in order to access the experience of their core. But when you have the experience it is only a full and complete experience if it is felt through the whole body. This brings us back again to the first principles of being grounded, being in our bodies and being calm. When you are doing something that feels really beautiful and connects you with your essence, see if you have the presence of mind to slow down and bring the experience fully through the whole of your body. To take a very normal example: next time you find yourself watching television in a very relaxed and comfortable way, just switch off the television, be aware of what you feel like and go deeper into the true relaxation.

Do whatever works for you. Soak in a candle-lit bath. Get a massage. Do whatever brings you beauty and let it all the way in. Letting it in, it then radiates from you. You are a blessing for yourself and for everything around you. To put it even more bluntly: be in a good mood and let the mood radiate the good vibrations of your core.

The benevolent energy field of the universe

The universe is also filled with vast energy fields of love and goodness. Yes, of course, there is negativity and a whole range of unpleasant atmospheres created by humanity over thousands of years, but human beings are only a tiny part of the universe. Our own clouds of negativity are tiny compared to the vast oceans of unconditional love, enlightenment, wisdom and ecstasy which permeate the whole universe. There has never been anyone who, on connecting with the energy and consciousness of the universe, has been depressed or upset. The universal mystical experience of the cosmos, from every religious tradition and culture, is one of love and beauty. The energy field of infinite space and all its levels of being is something we experience as love.

Everyone, at some time or another, has experienced this beautiful loving mystery of life. Usually we only taste it for a short while, but true mystics are connected to this beautiful energy field all the time. They have a continual awareness of what is beyond the human energy field. They connect into the vast vibrations of earth and universe.

We can all be mystics if only we remember to pause and give awareness to those moments of loving magic in our lives.

When we do blessing work, we choose deliberately to connect ourselves with the great benevolence of the cosmos and to channel it into specific areas.

The basic technique of blessing

When you are calm you radiate a pleasant atmosphere from your whole body and energy field. If you want, however, to put a blessing into a specific object then you need to focus your energy so that it can anchor down into the actual atomic structure of whatever you are blessing.

The most direct way to put a blessing into physical material is to radiate it through your hands. All over the world you will see people blessing objects through the radiation of the palms and fingertips. Blessing can be done from other parts of the body, but the hands are the most obvious and least line of resistance. Hands act as a natural conduit for physical vitality to carry a blessing.

In perfectly normal circumstances many people can feel a warm radiation coming from their palms and fingertips. Relax, close your eyes and put out your hands as if blessing the ground. You ought to be able to feel a very subtle heat or tingle coming from them.

If you then place your hands facing each other, like praying but an inch apart not touching, you may also feel an energy buzzing between them. Some people can even see this vitality shimmering between their hands in the same way that they can see the shimmering aura of a tree or vitality sparkling in the air.

If, on the other hand, you are not particularly sensitive to this energy, do not be concerned. Just get on with the blessing work *as if* you could feel it; over a period of time you will gradually begin to experience its reality.

Now, if you deliberately calm yourself, ground and relax into a good mood, you can purposefully radiate that good quality. You can also consciously guide the energy of the good mood through your hands and into any object.

This is the first easy step in blessing. Deliberately go into a good mood and channel the good vibration through your hands. This does not require a lot of time or preparation. Most people can switch into a good mood at will and hold it for a few seconds or minutes.

Whatever mood or state you are in, wherever you are, whatever is around you, just purposefully switch on a huge philosophical inner smile. This inner smile sits in your stomach, your chest and your head. Feel the warm change.

Try another simple exercise. Pick up any object that you would like to have a better vibration. Look at it with a friendly and warm attitude. Close your eyes, go calm and place yourself in that good mood. Let that mood radiate through your hands into the object. Hold the blessing for 15 to 30 seconds. Now release it.

You will have your own sense of how well the object absorbed your vibration. You may want to do it again several times. You may want to touch the object as you bless it or hold your hands an inch away from it. It is all experimentation as you find your own best way of working.

The heart area of the human body also carries a natural radiance that can be used for blessing. Sometimes I have placed an object I want to bless in my breast pocket and let it sit there for a whole day, every now and again focusing on the radiance of my heart into the object.

Embarrassment, fear and doubt

It is only by doing blessings that we get to feel confident about them. When first starting, nearly everyone has doubts about whether they are doing something real or whether they are just using childish imagination. Many people also feel embarrassed when they put out their hands to give a blessing, partly out of shyness and partly because they feel awkward doing something usually reserved for priests. Other people feel that they are not worthy to do something that is 'holy' and experience some shame; and yet others feel an instinctive fear of being punished by a church or temple for stealing power from the priests.

Blessing, however, is a natural act that belongs to all human beings and it should not be restricted to ordained priests of an organised religion. Energy and blessing are universal.

Connecting with greater energy fields of blessing

Blessing can be much more powerful if we positively draw on the great fields of benevolent energy in the universe. This means that you have to be able to make a deliberate connection with them and then hold this connection while you do the blessing. This is not difficult.

To make the connection is straightforward. To think of something is enough to make an energetic connection. Thinking of something places you in harmonic resonance with it. If, therefore, you guide your mind to think of the universal energy field of love, that is often enough to connect you with it. For some people the words God or Spirit are keys to connecting with this energy field. For other people it is easiest to make the connection through

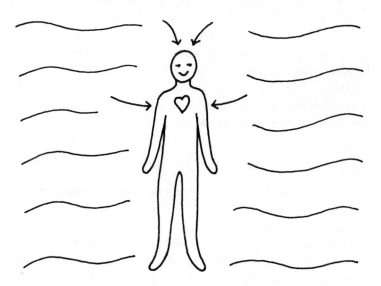

The universal energy field of love enters through the crown and heart

thinking of a particular spiritual being, place or symbol.

You will have to discover for yourself your easiest 'gateway' to connecting with the great clouds of good energy. What may surprise you, though, is that it is possible to make this connection very quickly and easily. It may not then be easy to hold the connection for much longer than a minute, but a few seconds is often all that you need to do a piece of work.

It is also much easier to connect with the energy fields of pure love if you focus through your heart and the crown area just above your head. I will explain why this is so shortly, but first let us review the basic method.

> Go quiet and grounded.
> Acknowledge whatever is to be blessed in a friendly and affectionate way.
> Switch on your good mood.
> Focusing in your heart and in your crown, you connect – either directly or through a helpful image – with the universal energy field of love.
> Bring it down through your body, into your hands and radiate it into what you are blessing.

There are also some simple exercises which can help you feel comfortable with this process.

Switch on a good mood, switch on connection

Above I suggested that you experiment with simply switching on a good mood. 'Whatever mood or state you are in, wherever you are, whatever is around you, just purposefully switch on a huge philosophical inner smile. This inner smile sits in your stomach, your chest and your head.' Do the same exercise, but this time, when you are in the good mood, also switch on a sense of connection with the beauty of the universe.

Switch on the good mood. Think how beautiful nature and the night sky are. Sense that there is love flowing through the whole universe. Switch on your connection with the benevolent universe. Try it. Just switch it on for a few seconds.

Draw on a beautiful memory

Another exercise helps with making the connection. You need to remember those times in the past when you felt a connection with sacred beauty and the deep wonder of life. It may have only lasted a few seconds, but the memory of those seconds is enough.

Take a few moments to recall one of those events. Remember all the details of how it felt. See if you can very gently experience those feelings again in your body. Relax, switch on a warm philosophical smile and let the warmth of the experience run all the way through you. In complete calm remember those times of great beauty. For this to begin to work, you must stay relaxed. Experiment with this exercise regularly.

Open your gateway

It is also useful to experiment with the spiritual gateways that work best for you. Take a few moments to think of a symbol, a place or a being that represents the divine and the beautiful for you. This may be a religious figure, such as Jesus or the Buddha or Mary; or it may be a symbol, such as the cross or five-pointed star; or it may be a sacred place, such as Iona, Glastonbury or some mountain with which you have a spiritual relationship.

Now close your eyes and relax. Switch on a good mood, switch on your inner philosophical smile.

Gently bring into your mind that spiritual symbol, place or being. Start with just the seed or hint of it.

Get an image or a sense of it. Make sure you are relaxed and grounded. Now gently place this sense in different parts of your body. If, for example, you are working with Christ, place your image or sense of him in your heart. How does it feel? Place it in your solar plexus or your eyes or above your head. You will find that the sensation changes as you move it around your body.

Do this exercise very playfully and gently, with no hint of stress or strain. The art here is to be focused in a very relaxed way with no knots of concentration.

The next step is to experiment with holding the image for a longer time period in the heart, above the head and in both of them at the same time. When people first work with placing an image in their crown, it often creates a feeling of strain around the eyes and sometimes a popping sensation in the top of the head. This is normal, so if it happens to you do not worry about it, stay grounded and keep breathing in a relaxed rhythm. It can be quite dynamic.

So, quiet and grounded, in a good mood, breathing gently, you place the image or sense of your spiritual gateway in either your heart or crown. See how long you can hold your focus while staying relaxed. Notice how it feels. Begin to sense a very real connection with this being and the energy field attached to it. Let the energy field come into your body. It will tend to come horizontally into the heart and vertically down into the head. For most people it is more comfortable to have the image sitting in their heart, though some find it easier to focus in their crown. Experiment with both.

You might perhaps begin to feel dizzy or day-dreamy or sleepy. This is the result of not being earthed properly, so go back to the exercises in Chapter 2 and

make sure you are grounded and in your body.
You will sense the energy entering and flowing
through you. You can increase the power of the
blessing by actively asking for and calling down the
energy through you.

For some people, the experience of doing this work can be
very powerful. For others it will be gentle and subtle. For
a few it may be so subtle that they may question whether
anything is happening at all; if you are one of this last
group, carry on patiently and notice the most subtle differences.

The reason for working with our hearts and crowns is
very specific. The human energy body is constructed in
such a way that it is easiest to link with the core self and
universal energies of love through the heart and crown. In
the same way that the area below the stomach is connected
with sexual energy, or the solar plexus with emotions, or
the brain with mental activity, so the heart and crown
connect most easily with transpersonal and spiritual
energies. It is simply the way that the human energy body
works.

Putting it all together

You can now put your blessing skills immediately into
operation.

Get quiet. Switch on a good attitude. Connect through
your gateway with the beneficent energy fields of the
universe. Allow and call in its energy through your
crown and heart. Let the energy down and through
into your body and into your hands, and bless
something.

Why not start by blessing a candle? As you allow the blessing to come through into the wax and wick, have a playful sense of each atom and molecule being filled with this new atmosphere of blessing. You need only do this for 15 to 30 seconds. You now have a candle which has absorbed the blessing. As you burn the candle, the blessing will be radiated continuously from the flame.

Or you may want to bless some incense, so that as it burns the blessing is carried by the scented smoke. Or bless the food you are about to eat or the water with which you might wash the floor.

Religious criticism and fear

The energy of the blessing will be coloured, of course, by the quality of the spiritual being with which you connect. Some religious fundamentalists may worry about the amount of free will that we can exercise here. They might make the accusation that we could just as easily invoke a connection with the devil as with Christ or Mary.

What they say is technically true. This kind of technique could be used to channel an unpleasant and negative atmosphere, except for one very important point. For blessings to flow, we must be grounded, breathing, relaxed and in a good mood. There must be no intensity or desire or ambition. The body must feel relaxed and good. In this state, with this attitude, it is impossible to channel a negative energy. The whole psychological foundation of blessing is a beneficent mood of love and goodwill.

The moment that any negativity or personal desire enters the situation, then the body will start to feel intensity and excitement.

The major lesson here is that when you do blessing work

you need to monitor two regions. First, monitor that your attitude is clean, moral and loving. Second, be sure that the body is relaxed and calm, with no tension running through it, especially in the stomach area or brain.

Religious fundamentalists may be frightened that, by working outside the limits of their strict religious guidelines, people will be led astray to do the devil's work. This is nonsense. People will, in fact, empower themselves and have a direct personal experience of love and goodwill; and they will choose for themselves how they get there.

Words, gestures and symbols of blessing

You can also enhance the blessing by using certain words and gestures which reflect the intention of what you are doing and complement it. For example:

'Connected with the spirit of unconditional love I bless this candle.'

'I place myself in resonance with the great spirit of love and bless this incense.'

'In the name of Christ' or 'I call upon the power of Christ to bless this object.'

'I surrender to the infinite ocean of the Divine Mother and radiate her blessing into this water.'

You should feel free to work with whatever words best suit your psychology and background. I recommend that at least you say out loud. 'I bless this object/person/space.'

Speaking it out loud adds to the power as the vibration of your voice helps carry the energy and intention. It also builds up self-confidence for this work. You may find that you are shy or stuttering, or even whispering like a mouse, when saying the blessing. This is a normal reaction to doing something new and risky, especially if you have any anxieties about religion. But I have seen many women and men find a new strength of character from daring to speak the words aloud.

Your hands can also make certain gestures to enhance the blessing. When the blessing energy is coming through your palms and fingertips, you may feel like moving one hand – usually the right hand, but the left hand if you are left-handed – to draw a symbol. Christian priests, for example, draw the sign of the cross over an object or person that is being blessed. People from a more mystical tradition in Europe may draw a five-pointed star. Jewish folk may use the Star of David. People with a more Celtic or tribal background will usually use an equal-armed cross, sometimes with a circle around it. People with a more Eastern background might draw the AUM symbol.

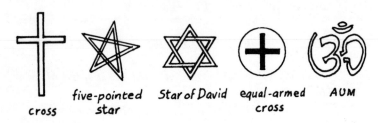

cross   five-pointed   Star of David   equal-armed   AUM
         star   cross

Universal symbols that may work for you

The use of these symbols draws extra energy into the blessing because these symbols are connected with vast reservoirs of energy built up over thousands of years. They work because, just like sound, colour and smell, shapes also have their own particular vibration. A shape vibrates harmonically with other similar shapes. The cross you draw in energy with your hand is therefore connected with a huge archetypal cross of spiritual blessing that exists as an energy field in its own right. When, for example, you draw an equal-armed cross with your hand, you connect with the archetypal energy field of the equal-armed cross: balance and earthed harmony.

This is why symbols also work effectively to strengthen bubbles and shields of protection. The energy that is brought through in blessing can also be used to enhance your bubble.

The best thing is to experiment with these symbols and to feel instinctively which ones work for you.

Holy water

In many traditions holy water is used to cleanse spaces, people and objects, particularly before worship. Properly made, holy water is one of the most effective cleansing agents that anyone can use. It is very dynamic and scatters stuck and negative energy. We use it regularly in our house when there is some kind of unfortunate atmosphere that needs shaking out.

Let me go through the basic procedure and then I will describe it in greater detail. The ingredients are a cup of water and a tablespoon of salt. You bless the water. You bless the salt. And then you mix the salt with the water. You then sprinkle it, using your finger or any suitable object, wherever it is needed. If you have children they love to do it.

The holy water holds its potency for a couple of days. After you have used it you can just pour it down a plug hole or scatter it in a garden.

Of all the cleansing agents that I use, holy water is in my experience the most potent – especially if it is made in the right way. It is worth, therefore, spending a bit of careful time making it. When I make holy water I use a fairly religious formula whose words are a bit gothic, but they suit me. As with all this work, readers need to find the way that suits them best, providing they stick with the basic format.

Here, blow by blow, is how to make holy water.

Place the two containers, one with water, the other with salt, in front of you. It does not matter what these containers are like. Travelling I have used paper cups, but I tend to like wine glasses or wooden egg cups.

Centre, ground and relax. Place yourself in a good mood, and focus in your heart and crown. With an inner smile connect with the vast ocean of cosmic love.

Place your right hand over the water and look with friendly affection at it. Then talk to the water as if it were alive and focus on its atomic structure. 'Creature of water, in the name of Christ, I exorcise you of all influences of evil and negativity, so that wherever you are scattered all evil and negativity may depart.' (If you do not relate to Christ, then use the connection with another sacred symbol to which you relate.)

While saying these words, draw the sign of the equal-armed cross into the water with your palm, feeling the energy imprinting these crosses in the water. Draw the cross as many times as feels comfortable. (If you do not relate to the equal-armed cross, use another symbol that works for you.)

Then bless the salt in precisely the same way. 'Creature of salt . . .'

Next take a pinch of salt between your fingers and sprinkle it carefully into the water drawing the sign of the cross. Sprinkle salt into the water this way three times.

Place both hands over the mixture and give it a final silent blessing, feeling the charge in every atom of the liquid.

You can, of course, use any words that suit you and any symbols that suit you. For example:

'In harmonic resonance with all that is good and beautiful, I channel a pure blessing of love into this water, so that wherever you are scattered there may only be love . . .'

'I surrender to the all embracing power of the Goddess, letting her divine embrace flow through me into this water, allowing no space for negativity . . .'

You can use no words at all if you like, but the basic procedure must be maintained: from an attitude of pure alignment with benevolent energy fields, you bless the water and salt using your hands, then mix the two together.

Holy water can be used anywhere. It can also be put into your bath when you need to cleanse your body or mixed into paint or washing water, so that the sparkling vibration is distributed around when you decorate and clean.

Here is a summary of what is needed for blessing:

- Be grounded and connected to earth.
- Be calm and breathing.
- Comfortably in the body.
- Switch on a good mood.
- Think of what is most beautiful and sacred to you, and connect with the universal vibrations of unconditional love and beauty.
- Make this connection particularly through the crown and heart.
- Draw the good feeling down into your body.
- Let it radiate through your hands.
- If you want to bless a situation, let it simply radiate from your whole body.

As you can no doubt understand, deliberately channelling a blessing is also a blessing for the person who does it. Whatever else may be happening in our lives, doing this kind of inner work brings us self-respect, a sense of service and an experience of love.

6

Happiness, confidence and success

Attitude and energy

To be an effective energy worker you need to be happy, confident and successful. It is no good switching into a mode of blessing for special occasions if the rest of the time you are moping around radiating a depressive atmosphere. Part of doing energy work effectively is to be a consistently good energy yourself.

This is difficult, especially as our society is a highly competitive place with five billion souls jostling for their place in life. From a purely material point of view – jobs and money – it does not seem possible for everyone to get what they want.

And if we cannot get what we want, how can we be happy, confident and successful? We are bombarded with images and experiences of what success looks like, and if our lives do not match these images we will be failures. Cars, houses, clothes, holidays, attractiveness, sexiness, power, influence, fame, status. Without them, what are we?

The reality, though, is that even when people achieve wealth and material success, most still do not feel happy. They are still anxious, still burning with nervous adrenalin, still competing and unhappy. I have spent several years researching attitudes to money and there were no instances of wealth creating happiness. There were lots of examples, however, of happy people becoming more happy with the extra freedom and choice money brought, but if they were not happy people in the first place, it made little difference.

A good experience of life does not, in fact, depend on external factors such as material success. It depends on what kind of basic attitude we have and this comes from inside. It is not given to us from the outside. We make a terrible mistake if we think that someone or something out there – a lover, a boss, a child, money, good looks – can make us feel happy, confident and successful. Perhaps external factors can temporarily make us feel good, but a good feeling that lasts is internal and personal.

Feelings and attitudes are energy. Happiness, confidence and success are energies. Because they are energies there are specific energy strategies you can use to bring them into your personality and your body.

Back to basics

The world of energies has completely different rules from the human social world. The world of energies has no interest at all in what you look like, how glamorous you are, what car you drive or how big your house is. It does not care where you were educated, or how rich or well-born you are. The world of energies cares about how you feel and the quality of the attitudes you radiate.

From this perspective a successful life is one in which you radiate more good than bad vibrations. It is the quality of your attitude and radiation that matters. It is *how* you do your work and conduct your relationships that really matters. This creates a completely different way of assessing whether you are doing well or not.

To maintain a good mood you have to come back to the basic techniques that are the backbone of this book. The logic is wonderfully overwhelming. It is absolutely impossible for you to feel happy, confident and successful unless you feel happy, confident and successful in your body. When we say, 'I feel happy' it is a complete experience. It is not partial. It is not restricted to the brain. It is an overall feeling.

The feelings of confidence and success are exactly the same. They are sensations that sit comfortably through the whole body.

It is impossible to experience any of these feelings on a consistent long-term basis unless you are first of all comfortable in your body. This means, once again, that you have to be grounded. You have to be in your body. And in situations of threat, you need to be able to breathe and hold your centre. The strategies for doing this are in Chapter 2.

In Chapter 3 you learned the strategies needed to deal with threatening external vibrations. But blocking your own sense of happiness, confidence and success, there are also inner threats you have to deal with. We all have inner shadows, thoughts and emotions that sabotage our feeling good, such as judgements, jealousies, worthlessness, victimisation and so on. These inner attacks can be dealt with in precisely the same way that you hold off outer attacks.

The very moment that you begin to feel self-doubt, self-criticism, insecurity and any of the other weapons of the inner critic, is the moment you need to ground, breathe, come to centre and work at being comfortably in your body. You will know when the inner critic is at work because you will lose motivation, your body will feel irritated and listless, your attention span will be short and your mind will keep wandering to other subjects; you will, in general, feel like escaping or falling asleep. Remember again the image of the trained martial artist, feet firmly planted on the ground, body energy securely located around the lower belly, breath gently even, face and eyes calm, attitude amused and philosophical. Can you think of any better tactic for dealing with the inner shadows that seek to disempower you?

Sometimes your negative feelings may be so powerful that it seems impossible to tame them, to ground and come to centre. You can always grit your teeth and count to ten as a first step. You can always take it 30 seconds at a time before you start to come to centre.

I ended Chapter 2 with a checklist that I want to repeat here.

- Be grounded.
- Be calmly in your body.
- Gently breathe.
- Be aware of your geographical location.
- Be carefully discriminating.
- Do it.

These elements are also the essential foundation for a general sense of well-being which supports you feeling happy, confident and successful. I am now going to deal with each of them separately.

Happiness

Healthy energy is energy that is moving. Where energy is stuck it always feels uncomfortable. Unhappiness is stuck energy. Happiness is a warm, moving energy. It is similar to humour.

I believe that humour, what makes us laugh, is when we

see energy moving and wobbling through something that we normally expect to be stuck in one particular mode. The stuck object can be a thing, a person, a situation, an idea or an emotion. A bishop slipping on a banana skin, for instance, is energy moving through an image that normally carries dignity. (Dignity is stuck energy, isn't it?) Forbidden and dangerous areas of thought become funny when new ideas send energy through them. Clowns are always sending energy through fixed ideas.

This is important because laughter is being increasingly recognised as a great healer and therapy. There is even a national health laughter clinic in Britain. Biochemically the brain releases natural chemicals of feel-good (endorphins) into the body when we laugh and these are felt through the whole system.

Happiness is humour toned down into a relaxed feel-good. Happiness is an energy that is always moving warmly and comfortably. Some modern mystics describe God as being like a friendly ocean of energy. Happy people are always grounded and fully in their bodies, and permanently connected to this warm, friendly ocean of energy.

Happiness does not detach you from reality. In fact, a paradox of true happiness is that it allows you better to look at and comfort suffering. Wisdom and compassion are the companions of happiness.

Energy needs to be kept moving through the whole human vehicle if there is to be this general feeling of goodwill. Warm energy has to be kept moving through the emotions and the mind just as much as the physical body. We know when this is working well because we feel relaxed and tolerant. Tolerance is a fluid and elastic energy field. Your goodwill does not evaporate when confronted with things with which you do not agree or do not like.

Happiness and tolerance are good friends. Tolerance as an energy is the opposite of frigid or rigid or inert or opinionated. Tolerance bends and flows.

If you are happy and meet negativity, you do not stop and freeze, nor do you fight back with negativity. You move your energy and attitudes in a flowing movement while you stay grounded and breathing – and you assess what to do next. This is the crucial element of happiness. You are warmly and comfortably in your body as you respond fluidly to whatever is happening. Energy keeps moving and doesn't get stuck in fear or hate or resentment. Your vibration remains positive and beneficent.

Physical rapport

Physically you have to be comfortable and accepting of your body, whatever shape it is in. Teaching energy work over the years I have found that it is crucial to like our bodies and have an affection for them. Your body obviously cannot feel happy if you do not like it. You must like and accept it. I know this may be difficult for people who do not like what they look like or who have painful disabilities. But I know for certain that you must have an affection for the physical vehicle that carries you around. This moves an energy of warmth and love through it.

If you are in affectionate rapport with your body, you begin to sense what it needs in the way of food and exercise. Usually it wants a healthy diet and regular exercise. What kind of exercise and what diet will depend on who you are. The exercise and the eating, however, must be done with enjoyment.

I do yoga, walking and swimming. They are of no use to me, however, unless I do them with enjoyment. If I do them out of a sense of duty and without affection, then I do not create happiness for myself. I might create fashionable trimness, but so what?

We have to enjoy how we move our bodies in order to get happiness flowing into them. We come back again to the attitude of possessing an inner smile. In fact there is a chi gung exercise which teaches us to smile inwardly at each of our internal organs for health and healing.

> In this exercise as usual you sit calm, grounded and centred. You then recognise that you possess an inner smile. If you want to, actually begin gently to smile. Feel an attitude of benevolence and affection gradually building within you. You are now going to give this affectionate radiance to your physical body and inner organs.
>
> You turn your focus inwards, as if you are looking down your throat into the great cave of your torso. From on high you are looking down on your inner organs. One by one – heart, lungs, liver, kidneys and so on – you greet each organ with a warm inner smile and wish it well. You sense its warm response and assess how it feels.

You have to keep your body moving with a warm attitude. I ask all my students to wake up each morning and to breathe awareness happily through their whole bodies starting at their toes.

Emotional acceptance

Emotionally you also have to be very careful not to let your feelings become stuck in one groove, but to keep them warm and moving. Some of you may be living in very difficult or oppressive situations, but you nevertheless need to affectionately flex and exercise your emotions.

First you need to fully accept and like your emotions, all of them. It is easy to like your sense of humour or generosity. It is not so easy to feel affection for your jealousy or hatred. Happiness and love are unconditional. They do not exclude anything. In the same way that you have to feel warmth for your physical body no matter what shape it is in, so you need to lovingly accept your emotions. In modern therapy and counselling, it is well recognised how destructive it is to deny the truth about ourselves. We have to accept everything. In this way the warmth of your awareness can circulate through all aspects of yourself.

Sit quietly and feel yourself fully in your body and grounded. Gradually take your focus down into the area around your solar plexus, just below the centre of the rib cage. Stay breathing gently and become aware of the emotion that sits within you. You are capable of anger and fury, and also of great peace and love. You can be jealous and you can be generous. There is security and insecurity. Gently become aware of the full spectrum of your emotions, from your very worst to your very best. Accept them and smile at them. Understand them as best you can. Embrace them. As well as constructing the foundations for happiness, this acceptance is also a powerful path of self-healing.

In physical exercise we stretch and move our bodies so that all muscles and tendons are used. We make sure the heart and lungs work. We try to achieve overall health. We also need to exercise our emotions. This means that it is healthy to feel the whole range of emotions, rather than just our usual old patterns. There is a whole range of emotions that we need to experience regularly: laughter, compassion, tragedy, sadness, elation and so on. You need, therefore, to do things that trigger these emotions.

Have you tried feeling emotions that are not your normal style? Have you tried romance or poetic sensitivity? Have you ever cheered on a football team? Can you feel tragedy and joy? Do you try watching films that are not your usual style? The great joy of Shakespeare, films, books, poetry, music, art and drama is that they stretch our emotions, taking us into new moods.

Listen to comedy shows. Watch tear-jerking movies. Listen to great music. Be present to wonderful landscapes. Notice the poor and needy. Focus on the starving children.

Stretch yourself by feeling all these different things, but be careful not to get stuck in any one of them.

If you have stretched into new feelings, then you will not be shocked or rigid when you meet them in unusual situations or when you are emotionally threatened. You will be able to keep goodwill and happiness flowing.

Exercise your mind

The mind is the most rigid part of our psychological structure. We love to cling on to what we think is right, whatever it is. Mental rigidity is the curse of our times. Good education and stimulating parents are supposed to teach us to have agile and fluid minds, able to move their way through all kinds of thoughts and ideas. In ancient Rome and Greece, the educated person was someone who realised that thinking was an on-going process which never concluded with a single correct answer. Correct answers which stop further thinking are boring and unhealthy. They are fixed ideas and attitudes which do not move. They are stuck mental energy. They sabotage happiness.

Get quiet and grounded. Focus your awareness around your throat and head. What kind of mentality do you have? Are you artistic or scientific? Sloppy or precise? Relaxed or rigid? Be honest with yourself and imagine what it would be like to have a different kind of mind.

Notice your thought patterns, projections, assumptions and judgments. Accept them all lovingly and then try thinking in a different way. For example, you may be very hostile to television and think that everybody watches too much of it and that it is destructive to society. Just for a few seconds, try the completely opposite attitude. Think, for example: television is wonderful. It gives everybody free access to the world. It is my relaxing window on the world.

On the other hand if you love television, try the opposite: I despise television. It destroys creativity and teaches short-span attention. The rays are physically dangerous and it encourages violence.

Exercise your mind properly. If you have been a conservative all your life, try thinking like a revolutionary Marxist. If you have been apathetic all your life and have no opinions, spend a while thinking fanatical thoughts. If you are religious, imagine being a humorous atheist. If you are an atheist, dream up arguments for the existence of God.

Keep your mental energy moving! One of the best things for shaking up the mind is to live in a completely foreign culture for a while. Sacrifice a small amount of your savings and go and live in a developing country. Get out of your culture and let your mind be stimulated by completely different ways of thinking and understanding.

If there is a subject that you will not let people tell jokes about, then carefully examine your pomposity. Relax. Chill out.

Do what touches your heart

Having exercised your physical, emotional and mental vehicles, make sure that you find the situations and energy fields which make you happy. If you love music, play it every day. If there is a certain type of tree that always touches your heart, grow one. If babies evoke your goodwill, then volunteer in a playgroup. Do what touches your heart.

There is also a general exercise that you can do. Get grounded, calm and breathing gently. Switch on a good mood and relax into it. Become aware of the energy fields of happiness and goodwill. Then, in a flowing way, imagine these energies circulating through your body – through your nervous and circulatory system; through the muscles and into the bones; sweeping and spiralling in the brain. Let these energies dance and flow through all your emotions. You will feel this especially around your solar plexus, chest and heart. Your emotions float in your aura, so have the moving energy sweep up and down through your aura. And do the same for your mind and your thoughts.

Here is another way of doing this. Remember the occasions and situations which have brought you love and a general feeling of contentment and comfort with the universe. Start with just a small thought and memory and see if you can experience once again the feelings that went with it. If something that feels good begins to happen inside you, then gently begin to turn the volume up on the experience.

There may be a particular place or person that touches your heart. Think of that place and person. Hold your attention in connection with that place or person. Feel your response and gently let the response grow.

Circulate the good feelings through you. Then ground, breathe gently and fully relax again.

Confidence

Energetically, confidence is a feeling of inner strength which endures regardless of circumstances. Genuine confidence is not rigid. It is not like a suit of armour which repels everything that touches it. Confidence is able to change its mind and opinion when faced with new facts and changing dynamics.

Genuine confidence, then, is like the strength of a tree. It is grounded and firm, yet it can bend without breaking and return to its original position.

There are very specific energy exercises which can help you achieve and maintain confidence. First, as always, realise that it is absolutely impossible to feel confident unless you are able to be calmly in your body. It requires that you are able to maintain your stable centre whatever other energies are coming at you.

Second, you need to be able to use, when necessary, the basic strategies you have learned for psychic protection.

Third, you need your energy field and nervous system to feel vital and strong. This strong vitality can be developed with a technique that is taught in many traditions, where energy is drawn into the body from the earth below and from the sky above.

These two streams of energy meet in the stomach and chest where they strengthen the ball of vital energy located in the lower belly. This exercise vitalises and strengthens the nervous system, so that you physically feel strong and confident. The strange or aggressive vibrations from the external world will not then wobble you off centre.

In Western magical traditions, this exercise is done as if you were a tree. Your roots go down through your feet and lower spine, deep into the earth, drawing up its energy. Your branches reach up high and wide, pulling and accepting the energy of the universe. The two streams of energy meet in your torso, the strong central trunk of the tree. Deeply rooted, reaching high

– absorbing the best of the earth and the universe into your very core.

When I teach this strategy in my own courses, I follow a chi gung approach and I ask my students to let their minds connect deep into the fire at the centre of the earth. They then sense themselves drawing up the energy of the fire into their bodies. They then take their focus up through their crowns and connect with a star – perhaps the Pole Star, or Sirius, or one of the Great Bear. Energy is then drawn down through the crown into the body.

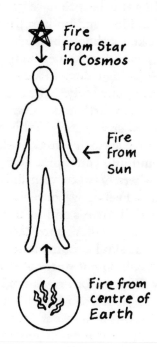

A third energy is then drawn in horizontally. This is the inner fire of the sun. Sense a connection between your solar plexus and the sun, and gently draw the fire of the sun directly into your stomach.

105

You thus have a threefold inflow of energy: the fire of the central core of the earth; the fire of the stars above; and the fire of the sun. You draw these three energies in simultaneously, let them meet in the region of the belly and feel a growing warm glow. As always you need to stay calm, relaxed and grounded as you do this exercise. There must also be a relaxed and good-natured sense of humour about this exercise, so that the vital energy is nurturing and easily integrated.

This exercise is best done standing or sitting in an upright chair. You need to have your spine straight. If you are standing it is best to have your feet directly under your shoulders and both of them facing directly forward. Your knees should be slightly bent, your shoulders back and your spine erect.

Get your breathing calm and sense yourself fully grounded and in your body. Now take your awareness deep down into the earth and become aware of the fire and molten metal and heat. Feel this fiery energy coming up from the earth into the soles of your feet, up your legs and into your spine and up your back. Let it settle somewhere between your lower back and shoulder blades. Feel its warmth and radiance.

Now lift your awareness and focus on the area a few inches above your head. You may feel a gentle popping sensation in your skull or some tension around your face and forehead; do not worry about this as it is normal. Now lift your focus even higher up into the sky and connect with a star high above you. This can be any star or it can be a star which you already know. Be aware that this star is also a great sun in its own right, radiant, nuclear and very powerful. Gently draw its energy down into you through the top of your skull and then down into the spine.

Bring the star energy down so that it meets the rising energy of the earth. Where they meet they dance, spin and fuse comfortably creating a warm radiance.

Direct this warm radiance so that it sits in your lower stomach.

Now let your awareness go out horizontally and connect with the great warmth and light of the sun. Be aware that there is an inner life to the sun with huge force and fire at its core and essence. Gently draw this fiery essence horizontally into your stomach and chest.

The sun energy now meets the energies of the earth and the star. Let them fuse comfortably and warmly. Let them sit glowing in your lower belly.

Now begin to circulate this energy through your body. Up your spine and head and then down your face, chest and stomach. Let it circulate in spirals in and around you. Take it through your blood circulatory system. Let it move through all your nerves. Into the muscles and tendons. Into the bones and marrow. Let it radiate generally through you.

Keep all this energy moving calmly and warmly. Stay grounded and keep your breathing gentle and rhythmic. Fully absorb the nurture and nourishment.

At the same time it is useful to repeat self-motivating affirmation to yourself, such as, 'I am strong and confident,' 'I have the perfect right to be who I am', 'I don't care if people disagree with me because I am a tree, strong and confident'.

Put at its most dramatic you then become like a solar deity, confident and radiant. This kind of confidence is caring and generous. It is an energy which supports both yourself and other people.

Done consistently and regularly this kind of exercise is immensely powerful. It helps you move beyond temporary psychic protection into a personal strength that is enduring. It does not necessarily do away with the need to gain education or experience. It does, however, provide a firm base for a new approach to life that can be a genuine blessing for everyone.

Success

Understanding the world of energies gives you a new way of assessing whether your life is successful. Success is not judged by material possessions or status. Success comes from an inner sense of integrity. You achieve this integrity when you know that you are doing your best to be in flow and in harmony with the energies of the universe.

This means that your general radiance is benevolent, that you do not pollute the psychic world. This means that, when called to, you actively do what you can to clear up and transform uncreative and inert situations. This also means that you give real awareness to allowing the consciousness and energies of your core self to come fully present.

If you are doing all these things, your life does not become static and correct. You are not sitting at a desk in some cosmic classroom waiting for teacher to mark you out of ten. You are part of a huge, ever-emerging universal flow of energy. Everything is always changing and moving. Your own lessons and moods and ways of being change as well.

A sense of inner success, then, comes from a very private inner feeling that you are riding the ocean of life in a way that is true and authentic for you. How we do this will vary from person to person. But the private inner feeling is the same. It is a quiet sense of correctness and calm. It is not complacent. It is looking for change and lessons. Even when you are going through very challenging times, perhaps even losing self-control or being frightened, you can come back to this inner place of quiet integrity.

How is it possible that you might lose self-control, yet still have this sense of integrity and success? Our histories and our wounds make it inevitable that there are areas in our lives in which we are very vulnerable and the inner child has not had space to mature. The inner child is that part of our psychology which holds all the fears and unfulfilled aspirations we had as a child. Although it is mainly in our unconscious, it nevertheless has a profound effect on much of our behaviour and much contemporary psychotherapy is devoted to healing the inner child. When this inner child breaks down or erupts this is to be expected and completely natural. It is unnatural if we repress and constrain it. It is also unhelpful and out of integrity if we let it repeat its angry patterns without beginning to tone them down and heal them.

We all have our own unique lessons and they will include inner friction and suffering. This is the normal way of karma. But they can happen in parallel with our inner integrity and sense of success.

A sense of success has much more to do with *how* we do things and not what we do. Material achievement never satisfies the inner self, unless the achievement is accompanied by a creative attitude and behaviour.

People often go into crisis trying to work out what they should really be doing. They go through a long process of soul-searching, scanning possible other work, asking friends what they think and generally winding themselves up into a state of anxiety. I have done this many times but every time I end up with the same answer and insight. It is not what I do that matters. My sense of frustration has nothing to do with what I am doing. It has everything to do with the kind of attitude that is radiating through my life.

These times of frustration are always signals that a change of attitude is needed. It is time to be more reflective; or loving; or creative; or dynamic; or supportive; to be more of a leader, or more of a helpful follower. My core self is asking me to change my vibration so that it can come in more fully.

There is a saying in the Chinese oracle, the *I Ching*, 'You may change the town, but the well remains the same.' You may change your external circumstances, but you still have to deal with the reality of your own personal energies.

Let me give you an example from my own life. I once lived in a tiny flat with my wife and crazy teenage son from a previous marriage. As you can imagine, the situation was uncomfortable and fraught. I felt a failure and that I had to get a bigger home, which required more money. I got caught in a mental frenzy of confusion as I tried to work out what to do next.

Finally, I began to assess what was really happening to me. The situation with my teenage son was triggering my own aggression and anger which I needed to heal. I needed to become more compassionate and understanding. As I realised what I needed to do and changed my attitude, so I began to feel at peace in the situation. My energy field became harmonious and the whole situation began to change. Having learned the lesson we then moved house.

The really important point is this. Supposing it had been absolutely impossible for me ever to get a larger home, as it is in many poorer economies. Supposing we had all been in a single room as many families on our planet live with no choice – then I might have carried on stewing and fuming for the rest of my life. I had to change my attitude.

I challenge all readers who blame their circumstances for their uncomfortable feelings to imagine that their situation is never going to change. You therefore have no alternative but to change your attitude. Some of you might find this idea outrageous because you are so accustomed to blaming external circumstances when you feel bad. But be realistic. If you were on a desert island or in a prison cell or on a mountain top, with no one to disturb you, do you really believe that you would pass through years with no bad moods and irritation? Equally, if you had a palace and a hundred perfect slaves pandering to your every whim, do you think you would also never have a mood or depression? Moods, irritability and depressions are part of our normal make-up. They need changing from within ourselves.

(And please do not interpret any of this as meaning that you should allow circumstances or people to abuse you. We should all know when to draw the line against other people's aggression.)

Here is a simple exercise. As always, come to centre, breathe calmly and feel your body and the earth. Then bring into your awareness some situation or person which has persistently over a long period irritated and distressed you. Now play an imaginative game. Pretend in your mind that you can never escape this irritating situation and that it is going to go on and on and on. In the middle of this irritating scenario, switch on an inner philosophical smile. Begin gently to accept the situation. Notice your resistance and ongoing irritation. Keep radiating your inner smile. Make sure your breathing stays calm and that your body feels relaxed. Then ask yourself a simple question: If I am to feel happy in this situation what positive inner attitude do I need to adopt? What negative inner attitude do I need to drop?

You may get immediate insights, but you might also need to do the exercise a few times in order to gain some helpful understanding into how you can change your attitude and feelings.

Success is also knowing that you have energetically helped the world. In the ancient Egyptian religion there is a wonderful myth that occurs in their description of what happens to us after death. Your core self or soul goes through a number of different learning temples. In one of the great temple chambers, your soul is weighed on a scale against a feather. Does the energy history of your soul carry the weight of negative atmospheres or is it light because of its service to the world?

Take a few minutes every day to assess the impact of your energy on the world. When you notice that your attitudes were unpleasant or selfish, it is possible to draw them back into yourself and reabsorb them. This is very similar to the classic exercise of breathing in negativity, breathing out blessing which I describe in the next chapter. Using precisely the same technique of feeling, absorbing and transforming the energy, you remember the scenarios of your bad behaviour and rework the energy. A perfect completion to this is, if possible, to apologise directly to the other people involved. Apologising is a powerful energy exercise because it draws back in negativity and creates a potential for a blessing.

Quietly assessing your difficult attitudes and behaviour is in itself a useful form of energy work, because the enlightened energy of the watchful mind is a powerful force for good. The 'light of the mind' casts energy into shadows and moves old energy. It has an illuminating effect simply by focusing on something.

Sitting quietly, happily and confidently, reflecting and contemplating on life in general, and on your own life, you direct illumined mental energy. This energy is like a soft laser beam. It penetrates and it shifts the shadows and the cobwebs of musty patterns. Letting your illumined mind thoughtfully ponder who and how you are is a distinct form of energetic cleansing.

Your ability to be attuned to the dance of your changes and to give enlightened awareness to whether you have radiated to the world for good or bad, this is the foundation of true success.

7

Evil, fear and advanced cleansing techniques

Evil as an idea and as a reality

If we are studying atmospheres and energies, it would be naïve not to focus on the subject of evil. This is a very emotional and charged topic, which is not surprising as it touches the most terrible experiences human beings ever have. There are huge differences in the way that people think about evil and many people do not want to give it any attention at all. To think or talk about evil and negativity, some argue, is to give energy and consciousness to elements that are best left alone. Other people – usually those who have never actually experienced it – reject its very existence.

But we do need to discuss evil because people meet it in their lives and people need to know how to handle it.

It is interesting how the main religions view it. Islam, Judaism and Christianity, for example, tend to recognise evil as a primal force which tempts us all, which we have difficulty resisting and from which we should defend ourselves with the greatest possible spiritual force. It even has a conscious agent directing it, the devil. And the devil has elemental spirits, demons, serving his will and even sometimes fully taking over a human life. This is indeed an unpleasant view of the world. Many people brought up in Christianity, Judaism and Islam carry these ideas in their subconscious. Even if they leave their childhood religion behind, they are nevertheless haunted by these ideas.

Other religions, though, have a different understanding of evil. Hinduism, for example, is more relaxed about it, recognising a wide variety of forces in the universe, including senseless cruelty and destruction. Evil is a natural part of the cosmic fabric and the human relationship with it will depend on our individual histories and karma.

Buddhism, on the other hand, tends to view evil as an aspect of human ignorance which can be transcended by an enlightened consciousness.

There are other belief systems which understand evil to be a necessary balancing force in the cosmos. Just as there is light, there needs to be darkness. There is nothing wrong, they might say, with this darkness. It is only human ignorance and fear which do not appreciate its necessity.

In occult and mystical teachings, however, there is a clear understanding that evil exists as an active force and that it needs to be purposefully countered with vibrations of light and love. These esoteric teachings, I have found, are difficult to understand when it comes to a clear explanation about the actual nature and source of evil.

Being frightened by an energy field which, for want of a better word, we call *evil* is not so unusual. There are very few people who have not at some point or another met a situation – sometimes in dreams – which has frightened them in a way that is unusually unpleasant. Sometimes we wake from dreams, from nightmares, terrified, and we know that the fear is not just from our own repressed anxieties but comes from some other force beyond us. Sometimes we meet people and we just know that there is something wrong, something beyond the normal bounds of criminality. Equally, there are places where the atmosphere is thick with a sick and frightening vibration. I have encountered them, for example, in Northern Ireland and they exist all across the world where there has been warfare, terror or torture. People in the Western democracies are generally blessed by rarely encountering these energy fields in buildings or the landscape, but if they travel to places of terror they soon discover them. Like mine fields, they need cleaning up, even after peace is declared.

Ever since I first became involved in energy work, I have tried to understand the energies of evil and in all my workshops I have always taken time to discuss the subject. For a long time I just listened to these discussions and then would simply suggest the most appropriate strategy for dealing with the situation. I did not fully understand what evil was, but I knew from my training and personal experience the various techniques for shielding and dismissing it. It is only in recent years that I have come to an understanding which partially satisfies me. Let me share what I understand with a clear caution that it may only be partially true.

Towards a definition of evil

It seems to me that what we call evil consists of two ingredients: a natural cosmic force and an energy created by human behaviour.

The cosmic force is easily recognised. It is the dynamic cycle of decay and destruction which we see in all aspects of nature. It is the normal rhythm of *all* life that there be death, loss of body/form and decay. The elements bound together to create a life sooner or later break down and disperse. This breakdown can be seen in plants, animals, stars and galaxies. There is a total inevitability about it.

This breakdown is usually accompanied in organic nature by smells and putrefaction, and we tend to find this process unpleasant. Few of us like to be close to rotting meat; we find it more attractive in the controlled environment of a compost heap. In the Hindu religion there is even a particular goddess who represents this aspect of the cosmic rhythm. She is Kali, a female deity of destruction and organic disintegration who finally devours everything.

The second dynamic in evil is the energetic effect of a certain kind of human behaviour. This behaviour is a tortuous destruction of life done with a sense of pleasure. It happens when personal resentment, anger and aggression hook up with the natural energies of decay and destruction.

We all of us have moods of depression, anger and destructive aggression. This is very human, but imagine for a moment that this mood – in a wild frenzy or in a situation of collective sickness – becomes connected to the cosmic dynamic of decay and destruction. This force of decay is universal and very powerful. It is possible to get lost in it and for our consciousness to be overtaken by it. Then, in the terrible cauldron of our own destructive mood mixed with the force of universal decay, we lose all sense of what is the right and of what is the normal rhythm of life and death. We become agents of thoughtless destruction and decay. The most nightmarish quality is that when people get caught in this state it seems that they actually begin to enjoy the destructiveness and inflicted pain. They become sadistic in a demented, pleasurable and infantile way.

As we know, this can result in the most awful of human behaviour: abuse, rape, torture and death to individuals and to groups.

This behaviour can surely be called 'evil'.

A working definition of evil, then, for me, is that it is destructive human behaviour mixed with the cosmic energy of decay and enjoyed by the perpetrator. It is destruction with no creative purpose.

Evil situations are also filled with the vibrations emitted by the pain and suffering of the victims.

There therefore exist in the psychic atmosphere of our planet large energy fields filled with the vibrations of evil behaviour. These clouds are powerful and sometimes overwhelming. They have an immense history. We need only think of the energy surrounding the Nazi concentration camps, or the killing fields of Cambodia, or the ethnic cleansing in Bosnia. Every time a child is raped or someone is slowly tortured this energy field is fed.

I am sorry to be so explicit, but we are dealing here with very real energies. In a book on psychic defence, cleansing and blessing, it would be inexcusable to ignore them.

So evil is an energy field that is very distinct from ordinary hostility or negativity. It does not pass easily. It is large, penetrating, seductive and powerful. Please be clear that it is very different from normal negative emotions or aggressive behaviour.

I reject, therefore, the Western religious idea that evil is an active cosmic force seeking to ensnare all of us. I also reject the idea that it is simply ignorant human behaviour. I believe and experience, however, that it is a powerful and deviant form of human behaviour which has created its own sinister force field.

Evil frightens us and it may also channel through us if we start to behave in a way that is harmonic with it.

All of this should be warning enough that we need to be very cautious and clear about it.

Dealing with evil

Because evil is such a potent energy field there is a universal procedure for dealing with it. Be strong. Push it firmly away. Do not get into relationship with it. Never try to start a communication or connection. (Do not ask evil home for a cup of tea in order to give it counselling.) It is too powerful. Shield yourself with as much spiritual force as you can and reject it purposefully.

If you ever meet evil, you will recognise the immense usefulness of being connected with the great energy fields of cosmic love and enlightenment. Drawing on the pure energies of Christ – or whatever great spiritual force you are connected to – you can shield yourself and direct a laser beam of spiritual power at evil.

I remember a real turning point in my own training in this work. I was learning how to enter transcendent states of consciousness in meditation. At the same time I was giving awareness to the political evil that exists in the world. (This is a training that teaches real-life compassion alongside cosmic consciousness.) And I began to have a series of dream experiences in which it seemed as if I were being attacked by energy associated with Nazis and fascism. The first few times this happened I could not control any part of my dream experience. I was extremely frightened and awoke in a cold sweat. It felt evil.

I then began to pray for help in my dreams when the attacks started. I withdrew my attention from the force attacking me. I did not try to engage with it. I envisioned myself surrounded by crosses and called upon Christ to help me. I used the classical techniques of psychic protection and I intensified my connection with the benevolent deity. I put all my concentration into connecting with Christ and Cosmic Love and bringing them down into my bubble and shields. At the same time I repeated over and over again the Lord's Prayer. This worked, I was still frightened, but less so.

Over the next year, I was attacked several more times, but was now becoming more centred and self-controlled. I began to gain courage and confidence.

Then one night I was attacked again. I drew up my shields, said my prayers, made my connection – and I felt completely protected. I felt so safe that I actually felt *dynamically loving* towards my tormentor. There was a huge field of love power around me and I now actively went towards my tormentor to fill it with this love. Of course, it now withdrew and I found myself chasing it with love. This was a glorious moment for me. I brought myself out of the dream state and into waking consciousness with a huge smile.

Following the basic rules of psychic protection and drawing upon the force of the cosmic energy field of unconditional love, I had gradually been able to build up my skills and strength. It was not a matter of blind faith. It worked because I had made genuine energy connections with a loving force.

That was an example of countering evil in a purely metaphysical setting, that of the dream state. There are professional carers I know who feel that they have encountered the same energy in hardened criminals and dangerous psychotics. Several doctors and carers have described how frightened they felt when working with certain patients and clients. Their strategy then was to put up all the psychic protection they could, make a connection with the strongest spiritual force they knew and radiate a creatively assertive love into the situation. I know a community nurse who will not enter certain houses without first taking five minutes to prepare herself. I know a businessman who sometimes feels the need to act in the same way before meeting other business people whose motivation is only power and greed.

Why we need the help of an external spiritual force

If we find ourselves dealing with evil or extreme negativity, it is usually necessary to draw upon the help of an external spiritual force. We need this outside help because we cannot rely purely upon our own moral force. This is partly just a matter of size. Some of the negative energy clouds are so large that we will be like small birds in a tornado. To counter the full force of the negativity we need an equal and greater beneficent power.

There is also a psychological aspect which is to do with your own unconscious. You may take pride, for example, in your strength of character and sense of morality, but there may also be dark areas of your character which are so old and deep that you are not fully conscious of them. These shadow aspects may resonate with similar negative energies outside of yourself. Or when you are frightened, these shadow aspects of your psyche may start to vibrate intensely.

If you are in a very negative energy situation you cannot afford to rely purely on your own resources, because you may be 'wobbling' too much internally. You must be connected to an external spiritual force.

I cannot imagine – nor have I ever heard of – anyone who works in this area not being connected to a beneficent spiritual force. It is crucially important, therefore, if you feel you are meeting genuinely negative force fields that you have a profound and unshakeable connection with pure Spirit. Then, when you are in a challenging energy situation, you can draw on this connection.

If you are in a challenging situation that frightens you, then you must make the connection in a very intense and fiery way. There must be nothing else in your mind except holding to your connection. Use all the usual techniques of psychic protection and at the same time be fiercely single-minded in affirming your trust in beauty, love and spirit. You may find it best to use a prayer that you like and repeat it quickly over and over again. Or you can make up the words that express your connection and use them repeatedly as a mantra. In my own experience the most beautiful prayer is from the Psalms of the Bible: 'The Lord is my shepherd . . . Yea, though I walk through the valley of the shadow of death, I will fear no evil: for thou art with me.'

Fear

In the same way that people find it reassuring to talk about evil and make their ideas and experiences conscious, people also find it useful and reassuring to discuss their experience of fear.

From an energetic perspective, fear is a vibration, not a psychological experience. The effect of fear is of course psychological, but the initial experience is caused by the uncomfortable vibration of two energy fields meeting in disharmony. I described this briefly in the first chapter, but it is worth looking at again.

Fear occurs when the human aura meets another energy field whose vibration creates friction with the human aura. Instead of a harmonic convergence which ripples comfortably through the human aura, down into the skin and nervous system, there is instead a spiky lightning fork of electricity which barbs its way down into the nervous system. This is an unpleasant experience.

If, however, you understand that fear is a sign that something is happening in your aura, then your reaction to it can be very different. When I feel fear now, I think: 'Aha, something interesting is in my energy field. Let me come to centre and see what's happening.'

When working with atmospheres the experience of fear should be taken as a signal that something unusual is touching your energy field. To put it another way: the moment that you feel fear, instead of getting lost in the experience, you should become observant about yourself and recognise that something unusual is happening. There is a genuine wisdom in the old saying that, 'The only thing we need to fear, is fear itself.'

The moment that fear is experienced, we need to enter into a state of mind that recognises the duality, the separation between body and consciousness. The body – its aura and nervous system – is registering the new energy. Our consciousness, however, can simply observe it without reacting to the experience.

At the first sign of fear, ground yourself and come to centre; switch on alert and detached mindfulness. In psychological language, do not identify with the fear. Do not buy into it. You can either keep a sane psychological distance from it or you can get lost in its sensation and panic.

To achieve the necessary detachment requires a brief act of will power.

In many traditions students are specifically taught how to be detached from the experience of fear. Some Buddhist monasteries regularly ask their novitiates to spend a week or more living and meditating, night and day, in a cemetery surrounded by corpses. Some readers may also remember the lessons of Carlos Castaneda who was directed by his teacher, the shaman Don Juan, to lie face down for the night on the side of a mountain and to do nothing, whatever he might experience.

In both of these examples, the student is learning how to stay centred while unusual and frightening vibrations happen in their auras. After a while, they learn to be dispassionate about these 'frightening' feelings in their aura. It is not a comfortable experience, but it brings a useful freedom.

This kind of work, however, is not everyone's cup of tea. I have found, though, that everyone is interested in this subject. Even if you are not going to practise it in any way, it is reassuring at least to know about it.

Advanced cleansing techniques

If, and only if, you have a calling for it and feel comfortable with the work, then there are some further cleansing techniques you might like to try out. Even if you feel comfortable, you need to self-assess whether you are in the right state of mind and physical health to risk situations that might make you feel some anxiety. If you are exhausted or highly strung, for example, then do not stress yourself further.

Breathe in negativity, breathe out a blessing

In Chapter 4 I wrote that healthy energy was moving energy and that usually it is enough just to get stuck atmospheres moving – using vibration, sound and aromas. Getting stuck energy moving is enough to transform it from an unpleasant and stagnant vibration into something radiant and good.

Sometimes, however, the negativity is so deeply coloured or ingrained that getting it moving is not enough to transform it. In these situations we may want, therefore, actually to cleanse and transform the quality of the negative atmosphere. The basic technique for this transformation is still taught regularly in the Tibetan Buddhist tradition, but any parent or lover who has ever held a distraught child or partner will be familiar with it.

In this technique, holding a perfect centre of grounded calm, you deliberately draw into your own aura and body the unpleasant vibration. You feel it running through your body and then, by holding a calm centre, you gradually absorb and simultaneously transform the negativity.

The negativity transforms because it is enveloped by your gentle calm. When you experience its pain or anxiety, instead of letting it rush through your body in an anxious sigh or movement of distress, or instead of holding it uncomfortably until it releases in a scream or a shudder, you breathe your tranquil consciousness through it.

At the same time therefore that you absorb the negativity, you also radiate love and goodwill into it. Sometimes you find yourself absorbing the negativity for a few minutes before you begin to bless it.

This is a very similar experience to holding a screaming child, absorbing its trauma, gently calming it down. Obviously it is crucial when using this technique to feel genuinely confident and calm.

N.B When starting this kind of work, *always start in a small and humble way*. Do not try and fix everything in one go. You may be overwhelmed. Always start with just the tiny seed of an intention. Sense the negative situation very tentatively. Only as you begin to feel more confident should you increase your experience of the negativity. If at any moment you begin to feel nervous, close yourself calmly down and stop the exercise. Do not ever do it unless you feel strong, calm and confident. And you must be fully earthed, comfortably in your body and in full tranquil control of your breath.

Breathing in negativity, breathing out blessing is a technique that can be used very beautifully every day as an act of service to your home, community and workplace. If practised every day for a few minutes, over a year or so you will feel the atmosphere of your neighbourhood changing.

We once moved house into an area of London where the local police station was renowned for being the most corrupt in Britain. From my study on the top floor of our house, I could see the back of the police station. Twice a day for three years, when doing my meditation, I would take my focus into the police station, particularly into the overnight cells, and connect with the stress, violence and general psychic mess that were sitting in the place. Having made the connection, I would then draw all the negativity out of the police station and into my own aura and body, gently sitting in it and transforming it.

It was not pleasant, but it was not that bad. I then sent thoughts of support and blessing into the station, wishing the officers respect, strength and a sense of justice as they did their work. As it turned out, over those years the police station did clean itself up and grow a better reputation. I do not know how much my work helped. It certainly did no harm.

Let me go through the technique a final time to make sure it is clear.

Make sure you are calm, grounded and breathing.

Make sure you are connected to the benevolent forces of the cosmos.

Very gently and in a small way, make and sense a connection with the negativity.

Not being overwhelmed, always strong, get a sense of your body drawing in the negativity. Feel it.

Stay breathing and calm. Have a benevolent smiling attitude. Stay centred.

Breathe loving and beneficent thoughts and feelings

towards it and into it.

Release your focus on the negativity and stay for a while in the glow of the good force of the universe.

If, when you have finished the exercise, you feel some energy stuck in you, move your body physically, give yourself a good shake and make releasing sounds.

I repeat that if you have any fears that it is not appropriate for you, then do not try it. If you are nervous but would like to have a go, then try it in a very tiny way for just 15 seconds. Review how it feels before doing any more.

One more warning. Do not use this technique for situations that are huge, evil and overwhelming. You may simply connect with something with which you cannot deal. Work with practical situations that personally concern you. Do not try and clear up a war zone. A friend of ours, for example, who was not very well grounded but very romantic and enthusiastic decided that he wanted to clear up the energy field of the Ku-Klux-Klan. He was ill for several days as he came back to centre after a very unpleasant experience.

Be reasonable.

Letting the Earth absorb the negativity

There are other approaches for dealing with generally negative atmospheres in particular places. The earth herself can help us. We often forget what a thin film of life we are upon the surface of the earth. And we also forget what a huge and magnificent creature of energy she is. The movements of the great ocean tides, the changes in temperature from dawn to dusk to dawn, and the changes in atmosphere through the sequence of the four seasons, all of these hint at her energy. She is also a great magnet, the power of which holds us all to the ground, and her atmosphere, surface and depths are filled with energy, magnetism and electricity. She can, therefore, absorb negativity deep into her body and circulate and vibrate it into a healthy form.

> The basic strategy here is to imagine and sense that in the centre of the space to be cleansed is a spinning plug-hole down which the negative energy is sucked away. You then get a sense of the energy actually draining away down it. (As a matter of goodwill and as a way of coming into relationship with the earth, I always ask her first for permission to work in this way; and I always thank her afterwards.)

This technique is particularly useful when groups of people have been discharging a load of emotion and pain, and the space is filled with their psychic discharge. In fact, I often lead groups in a visualisation exercise in which we all co-operate to have the energy go like water down the plug-hole. (And there is always some joker who makes the appropriate noise.)

Lifting the violet sheet up to the cosmos

This strategy is more difficult, but many people have been surprised by how effective it is.

> In this technique, you imagine and sense that there is a very large violet coloured sheet stretching out on all sides beneath the area to be cleansed.
> You then sense and guide this sheet into slowly rising upwards. As it rises, like a net, it catches all the unpleasant vibrations. It will feel as if the sheet sags elastically in the centre where it is holding all the stuff.

This is usual. Just gently persist – it may take two to ten minutes – until the sheet lifts fully up, now carrying its load.

You can now do one of two things. Either guide the sheet up into the centre of the sun where all the crud is furnaced and transformed. Or call in an invisible helper to take the sheet away. When I call in a helper, I imagine a 2-mile long Chinese luck dragon high up in the sky, with a deep resonating vibration, which is happy to absorb the negativity.

Angelic help and negative beings

Angels appear in the religions and mythology of all cultures in all religious periods. They are called by many different names and are explained in many different ways. In the West, some of them are called angels and certainly the three major Western religions openly accept and call upon angelic help. In fact, the Pope only recently confirmed the existence of angels as messengers of God.

Throughout the ages, people doing energy work have found that they can call upon the help of angels to transform atmospheres and co-operate in difficult situa-tions. If you feel so inclined, experiment with asking for their help. Providing you stay grounded and keep your bullshit antennae switched on, you can do yourself no harm.

There are also beings or blobs of consciousness floating around that have absorbed some of the energy released by evil and negative human behaviour. Associated with negative situations they sadly fully absorbed the patterns of negativity. These 'blobs' do not work with a deliberate negative purpose, but are drawn to situations which magnetically attract them.

They are attracted to situations of negativity and also to situations of spiritual growth. Religious history is full of biographies of people on the spiritual path who, while totally dedicating themselves to the divine light, found themselves tormented by devils and demons. It seems reasonable to explain these occult attacks, not as a deliberate attempt to sabotage spiritual progress, but as being attracted to the saint's own shadow.

As you move along the transformational journey – no matter how much your consciousness expands or you connect with love – your old shadows must be transformed. As they surface to be worked on, they attract resonant external energies.

The path of transformation, therefore, involves not only dealing with your own inner shadows but also resonant external shadows.

There are two basic strategies for dealing with external blobs. In both of them you need to go into a very calm and stable state. Once you are calm and quiet, ask the highest source of spiritual benevolence to help you and ask for angels to come to take the blob away. To call in this external help is not difficult. Go quiet and simply bring into your mind the idea of an angel. It does not matter how incomplete this idea is or what form, if any, it takes. Then aloud or mentally, say the words: 'I invite in and welcome the help of the angelic forces to aid in this situation. Thank you for being present. Thank you for your help.' Stay grounded and centred, and clearly hold the intention. If you have never asked for help like this before, you will be surprised by how effective it is.

The second approach is to let the blob fully into your own aura, embrace it with an attitude of unconditional love and transform the negativity in your own energy body. This is essentially the same technique as breathing in negativity and breathing out blessing. In this case you are working with a specific entity rather than a generalised energy field.

Ghosts

People often ask what they should do about hauntings. A ghost is a dead human being, without a body, who has not found their way along one of the energy paths that take them fully through the death and rebirth learning process. (See, for example, *The Egyptian Book of the Dead* or *Tibetan Book of the Dead*.)

Unless you are personally familiar with one of these paths for the dead, then go into an attitude of deep compassion for the poor earth-bound soul. Send it much love, sympathise with its experience and then ask the highest source of spirituality you know to send angels to help the soul on its way. You can make up the prayer as you go along and it needs to carry very clearly the meaning of what you want to happen. For example: 'Dear God, Dear Angels, Dear Supreme Power of the Universe, look with love and affection upon this poor earth-bound consciousness who should now go on its way. Help it move forward on its path. Take it upward into the light. Surround it with love and understanding. Draw it onwards to where it needs to go. Take it beyond this earth plane into the next realm of consciousness where it should be. Let your love enfold it and all be well.' Hold the intention of this prayer for anything up to 30 minutes. You may have to do this more than once until you feel that the atmosphere is clear.

Of course, while you do these techniques you can also use the other strategies of protection and cleansing which we have already discussed. With both negative beings and phantoms, holy water and cleansing incense are very helpful.

If you really want to get engaged with spiritual ecology, then you can meditate and pray every day, drawing in the negativity of your neighbourhood and sending blessing into it. At the same time you can begin to sense building up a helpful vortex of energy that naturally attracts all the blobs and lost phantoms in your area. This vortex then lifts the 'lost' beings up into the light and onwards on their true journey. This type of vortex may take a year or so to construct successfully, and will require daily attention. But if you are attuned to this kind of work, it can be of great service.

8

Spiritual rules: attitude, karma and grace

Personality and essence: the duality

We are dualistic creatures. We have personalities and we also have our essence, our core. Sometimes our personalities and our essence fuse. Sometimes they are very distant.

The personality is capable of creating a huge range of atmospheres and energies, reflecting our varying moods – from hate and distrust, through to love and affection. Over many thousands of years the aggregate moods of humanity have created huge clouds of emotion and thought surrounding our planet.

Our core self, on the other hand, is not entangled with human moods but has a distinct wise and loving vibration of its own, and is permanently connected with the universal energy fields of beneficence.

To get a clear grasp of how we work with energies and when it is right or wrong to intervene in a situation, we need to understand this strange duality in all of us. We have personalities which will radiate anything, depending on our mood, and we have these inner selves which radiate a blessing if we allow them through.

If we appreciate this duality within us, it leads to a very

obvious conclusion: from an energy perspective, our main purpose in the world is to radiate the blessing of our core selves, and to do what we can to transform the negative vibrations we and others have created. Whatever else we do with our lives, in the world of energies and vibrations, our task is to radiate blessings and clear up negativity.

Our invisible connections

There are huge religious and philosophical arguments about this duality between our core consciousness and our personality, but there is general agreement that the ultimate goal is for the two of them to fuse and integrate. This agrees also with much modern psychology which states that the purpose of human life is to fulfil ourselves; which means that the core self has to come fully present and not remain hidden behind the personality's patterns.

Described energetically, the purpose of human life is for the energy field of the core self to meet and integrate with the energy field of the personality. The personality then becomes fully coloured with the energies of wisdom, enlightenment and love. This is a pretty good goal, isn't it?

We are held back from fulfilling this goal by the energy field of our emotional and mental patterns, our habits and addictions. This is made even more difficult because all our personality energies are connected. We are not little islands going about our business separately. We are all connected through our energy with each other. This means that one person's bad attitude effects everyone else, just as one person's good attitude is a blessing for everyone else.

Even more intimately, we are linked through harmonic resonance with people who have similar personality patterns to ours. If we are selfish, we are linked harmonically to other selfish people. If we are aggressive, we are linked to other aggressive folk. Equally, our loving and generous qualities also link us with similar people.

This interdependence, long known to mystics, is also being realised today in modern science.

All of this creates a background to understanding our energy work. We never work in isolation, but are always connected to the whole human community.

The power and influence of the personality energy fields

There is a further reality which also affects us dramatically. Seen psychically the general atmosphere of our planet, created by humans over thousands of years, is a circus. *Everything* that has ever been thought or felt has left its imprint somewhere in the psychic atmosphere. There are huge clouds of psychic emotion and thought floating in the atmosphere. Remember that when someone feels or thinks something, the energy put into the feeling or thought continues to exist.

The psychic aura of the planet is a direct reflection of how humanity as a whole has felt and thought over hundreds of thousands of years. This is both an amusing and a distressing idea.

Our personal auras are in continual contact with this psychic kaleidoscope and we are continuously affected by it.

This means that when you are dealing with your own patterns and energies, you are also dealing with all the other resonant energies floating around. When you are working on your own stuff, you are also always working on the collective energy of humanity. You are also, of course, profoundly influenced by it.

Let us take as an example a very personal paradox. Even

if you feel isolated and separate, you are nevertheless energetically connected with all the other lonely people and with the great 'lonely-and-rejected' energy field created by lonely and rejected people over thousands of years. In exactly the same way, when you feel elated and amused, you are connected with others in the same state, and with the great energy field of 'elation-and-amusement' created by others over millennia.

This often means that when you are feeling powerful emotions or thoughts, you are not feeling stuff that is simply your own. You are feeling your own stuff – but you are also feeling the stuff of the collective.

In my workshops there has often been an audible gasp as people realised how affected they have been by external atmospheres they thought were purely their own. People realise that they have been expressing or channelling not just their own emotions and thoughts, but also those of the collective psychic world.

How can you tell whether it is just yours or whether you are connected to the collective clouds of feeling or thought? My own observation is that when we become connected to the collective energies, our feelings and thoughts take on a dramatic and theatrical quality.

This can be seen very easily, for instance, with anger. One moment we may be simply angry, expressing our own genuine grievance and fury. The next moment it has gone out of reasonable control and is expressing itself with an almost unstoppable fury.

It can also often be seen when sadness and self-pity move into hysteria.

Or it can be seen when religious preachers suddenly take off into a whirlwind of charismatic inspiration, as their own passion is overtaken by the great energy field of certainty and fundamentalism. You can also see it in politicians when a speech moves beyond the stability of personal passion to become a flow of fanaticism. In fact, a moving public speaker is precisely someone who can channel the feelings and thoughts of the crowd. Successful pop bands also often do the same thing. In fact, in classical theatre, in sacred drama, this ability to channel external energy fields is deliberately used to create atmospheres as the actors and actresses portray gods and goddesses at cosmic work and play. In the right costume and with the right words, they channel the archetypal energies they portray.

Our moods anyway connect us vibrationally with other similar moods. As we become theatrical, we open a gateway for the collective energy to express through us.

The best that you can do to avoid acting as the channel for the mass mood is simply to be self-aware. This is easier said than done when you are overwhelmed by your feelings, but simply knowing about this energy reality is the beginning of self-awareness and wise self-control. The best you can do perhaps is to monitor yourself after extreme moods and assess how much was actually yours, and then commit yourself to a lower volume next time. Simply understanding these realities may be enough to help you change.

You will also understand how important your own personal behaviour is. Your moods and thoughts do not simply affect you and those closest to you. They affect everyone. Equally, your self-control and transformation works to everyone's great benefit.

Being open to the core self

Personality moods, like depression, jealousy, happiness, affection, humour and so on, are very obvious to us. We notice and feel them very easily. In fact we feel them so easily that they can take us over with little difficulty. Anger, need and jealousy, for instance, can punch one in the stomach. Desire and attraction physically draw the body. Ideas and thoughts whirl in the mind, sometimes creating headaches.

It is less easy to notice and stay in the moods that come when we are connected to our core selves and to the beautiful dimensions of life. The energy of the core self and of the sacred is more gentle. Our usual behaviour, in fact, when we experience those moments of true connection with our essence and the universal essence, is to grunt and move on. We see a beautiful sunset or feel the atmosphere of a magical landscape, we stop for a moment, then we just move on as if nothing had happened. We can be transported to this beautiful connection with essence by sex, or art, or dance, or caring, and then move on, forgetting it.

A metaphor I often use is that the personality energies are like water and the energies of the core self are like a feather floating on the surface. In order to feel the core self more fully the water has to thin or have the right currents to allow the feather to float down.

If you seriously want to do energy work that serves you and the collective, then you have to become more efficient in letting through the energies of your core and of universal goodness. The greatest energetic good you can do is to bring through as much blessing as you possibly can while living a normal, grounded and integrated life. This means that you need to hang on to the awareness and the feelings you have when you are connected to essence. Let me give an example and I will use sex because most people are interested in it.

When a couple are making love, and there is affection and beauty happening in the love-making, it is very pleasant to stop all the physical movement and be fully conscious of the beautiful energies that are being felt. This allows even more good energy to come through and radiate. Never-ending physical movement can ignore that wonderful tantric energy.

Here is another example. If you are deeply touched by a sunset or some landscape, instead of walking on, you can stop and spend a while breathing it all in. Stopping and being in the atmosphere allows the energy to come fully through.

Here is one more example: many people, when caring for someone, find that they sometimes experience a genuine transcendent love. When these moments happen it is good to give them full awareness, and to let the atmosphere and blessing come fully through.

We need to be more attentive, carefully listening, receptive and absorbing the energy field of wisdom and love which is at our essence. When you feel those magical moments of connection with your core, then you need to stop and be fully present to them. You need to give the moment full awareness. You hit wondrous moments and let the moment slip by without absorbing the full atmosphere of the moment, without letting the quality settle fully into yourself, without letting the feather of your soul slip deeply into the water of your personality. You get touched by something sacred and religious, and then shut down instead of opening.

You have to put some effort of consciousness into connecting with the good vibrations of your core. By slowing down enough to give them awareness, you let them in more fully and you become a conduit for them through the whole of your life.

You can also purposefully create your connections with the sacred. In the techniques for blessing, we learnt how we can easily switch on a good mood and switch on our connection with universal beauty in order to channel a blessing. What I am encouraging here is that you expand your ideas about blessing. Instead of switching on the connections for the particular purpose of blessing a specific object, person or situation, it is worth contemplating the possibility of switching it on more regularly as a daily practice. It can be a way of life.

Duality, suffering and karma

The greatest of all spiritual ideals is that our personality completely integrates with our core self in what is sometimes called the 'mystical marriage' and we produce good vibrations all the time. The difficulty with being human is that it is not easy to do this.

Each of us has a different set of psychological circumstances with which we struggle. We are none of us the same. We have different histories and characters. It is impossible, therefore, to look at people in general and say: in order to achieve the mystical marriage you must all do this! Believe this! Follow this path! We do not all need the same things. There are different horses for different courses.

It is crucial that we understand these two fundamental points if we are to understand some of the rules for energy work. The two points are: first, our life purpose is to merge and integrate the personality energies with the energies of our core selves, but this is difficult work. Second, we all have different characters and histories so there are no universal solutions that work for everyone.

Take, for example, two people who are shy, timid and passive. For one of them it may be absolutely perfect that he remains like this, because in his unique circumstances this creates the best energy circumstances for the core self to come in. Maybe in the past, he was far too aggressive. The other person, however – because of her long history of victimisation – might need to become more assertive and dynamic.

There is a unique dance in every one of us between the

personality and core, and we can never generalise about what is needed. In many Eastern spiritual traditions, personal growth is understood to be like a river or an ocean with ever-changing currents, depths, temperatures and intensities.

It is also clearly understood that the patterns of the personality often resist the energies of the core self and that the experience of this resistance is very painful. Where there is resistance between personality patterns and core energies, we experience psychological tension and suffering.

This means, paradoxically, that we experience suffering when we are perfectly on our paths of growth and doing all the right things. It is important to understand this strange human paradox: that because we are doing the right thing we also experience the suffering of inner friction. This inner friction is the exact process by which we transform inner negative patterns into something more relaxed and loving.

This means that in our work to bring through good vibrations we may well find ourselves experiencing psychological pain. Tibetan Buddhists have a great attitude to this. Yes, they smile, it all hurts. So what? That's just the way it is.

Anyone who has given up smoking, or started a diet, or decided to be nicer, has experienced the resistance of the personality patterns. Patterns often hang on. Not only do they hang on but they come into friction with the energy of the core self.

The word *karma* describes precisely that inner friction which occurs when the energy of the core self meets the resistant patterns of the personality. The intensity of the resistance to letting in our essence is our karma. Behaving better we make it easier for our essence to manifest and our karma lightens. Behaving badly makes it more difficult for our core selves to manifest and our karma – the intensity of resistance – increases.

If we behave badly then we feed negative energy into our patterns, which makes them even more resistant to our core energy. If we behave well we feed benevolent energy into our patterns which makes them meet the core self more harmoniously. Bad behaviour creates greater pain for us. Good behaviour makes our changes easier.

But if we behave badly, we also radiate bad energy into the atmosphere. This negative vibration also carries the quality or the 'signature' of the person who radiated it. Therefore, as we transform patterns, we have to absorb and transform the old negative energy we radiated. This can be easy or very difficult. We have to work off, burn through or melt our karma. Our karma is the result of long histories. We all have it. There is no one without it.

Working with energy to help people and situations, it obviously helps to recognise that karma is present. Karma does not usually allow for miraculous interventions. Every individual has to clean up their own history.

Collective karma

All of this raises the question of whether we can ever do energy work to lighten someone else's karma. Can we really ease someone else's suffering? Mystics and religious philosophers can argue about this intellectually. From the heart there can only be one answer: we must always do what we can to reduce suffering.

Some cynics, however, may say that we should leave everyone alone to deal with their own karma. At their heartless worst these cynics may look at the death of the Jews in the Holocaust or the dying children in the developing world, and say that they asked for it. Its their fate. 'It's their karma.'

But this in no way recognises that every individual is part of a far greater dynamic which is the unfolding history of humanity as a whole. We have already discussed the collective feelings and thoughts that float in our psychic stratosphere. Humanity as a whole also has its shadow, its terrible history and its karma.

Individuals get caught up in this regardless of their individual history and karma. In reality, the individual is frequently the victim of mass events. An international war has far greater momentum than any one person's karma. Individuals often cannot avoid the natural power of famine or earthquake. Some people may karmically deserve it and a few may karmically avoid these great forces, but most of us are subject to the groups to which we belong. We cannot avoid our powerful links. No individual woman is free, for example, of the collective danger to women in city streets at night. Individuals are overwhelmed by racism and tribal emotion which is none of their making.

We have to understand that much of human life can be understood as part of a collective dynamic. A compassionate understanding of these realities means that there is always room for us to aim to relieve another's suffering and karma, but there are definite guidelines for when and how to intervene.

Rules of intervention

There are two general pieces of advice when it comes to doing energy work that affects someone else.

First, in general, mind your own business and do not intervene unless you are asked to by the person concerned.

Second, if you do intervene, then you must make absolutely certain that your personality is perfectly aligned with your core self and that your personal energies are completely relaxed while you do the work.

People sometimes do not understand why, when they have learned how to bless or cleanse, they cannot just go around blessing and cleansing everyone and everything. It is obvious, isn't it, that every individual has special needs and, unless you have universal wisdom, you need to be careful about what you are doing with energy. I have been in situations where complete strangers have come up to me, placed their hands through my energy field and without warning given me a blessing. I felt zapped, rather than blessed. I had not given these people permission to do this. They were not grounded, centred and calm. They were perhaps fulfilling images of themselves as helpful saints.

How could they know whether or not their blessing would be helpful for me? Never bless someone unless invited, and unless you are perfectly calm and aligned with the energy of your core consciousness.

There is the very practical issue of whether the person you are blessing is in a fragile physical state, for example with a heart or nervous condition. The sudden influx of external vitality might then be positively dangerous. A blessing always carries energy, especially if it comes through the hands. So it is most important not to be careless about blessing people who are ill. Teaching this kind of work, I do not want to be responsible for any thoughtless abuse.

There is, however, a form of energetic intervention that is always perfectly safe. You can send love and good energy to anyone, and into any situation providing that you do it from an attitude of perfect inner peace. You need this absolute inner peace because otherwise you will be radiating vibrations coloured by your personality. You do not want to send personality energy.

If you are grounded, in your body and gently breathing, if you are serene and watchful from your centre, then you can be certain that none of your personal energies will get involved and disturb your radiance of purity.

Let me give you two examples of when people are frequently tempted to do energy work, but in an inappropriate way. We often get upset when a close friend or relation is sick. We also get upset by large-scale conflicts in the world. We therefore have an understandable emotional reaction to fix the situation. We want to send healing blessings to our ill friends. We want to radiate peace into war situations.

The problem here is that we may simply send our own emotional energy that wants health and peace. Get better! Be peaceful! Our underlying unconscious purpose is to make us feel better when confronted by something which disturbs us. So we send our desire for healing and peace. This is, in fact, an emotional energy belonging to our own personality needs. We do not realise that we are also radiating our own concern and worry into the situation. We may make the situation worse.

In fact, our friend may need to go through the illness as a lesson and our concern just makes things worse. We may actually be radiating unhelpful energy even though we think it is creative.

Even radiating peace into a situation can be unhelpful. 'Be peaceful' can be an aggressive whingeing idea that only makes the energy conflict worse. Perhaps the situation does not need an imposed energy of peace. Perhaps it requires playfulness, or understanding, or release – for perhaps it genuinely requires the breakdown of old forms, even though the terrible cost is war.

It is often better to keep our worried prayers to ourselves and to get on with the practical work such as providing aid relief.

There is a Tibetan saying: 'Inner peace, universal peace'. If your own desire for someone else's healing or the cessation of warfare is based purely on your own emotional reaction to the situation, then it is very difficult for you to radiate a creative energy. It is absolutely crucial, therefore, that you go into a personal state of genuine inner peace before you do any energy work to bless a situation or a person.

It will always do good if you radiate a genuine peaceful acceptance and love. This is the energy of your essence and of the benevolent universe. It will be absorbed into the situation at the level of the core self and filter down into the personality realm according to the needs of the situation. When you want to send a healing blessing to a friend, be absolutely tranquil and think of your friend's core self. From your essence send love and blessing to their essence. Do the same for situations of conflict. This is the most effective way to work.

> Blessing a situation at a distance, therefore, requires the same opening strategies as any energy work.
>
> Get grounded, be in your body, calm breath, connected with your core and energy fields of universal benevolence. Sitting in this warm atmosphere, you can spend a while contemplating the person or region in trouble. *'Holding* the situation in love' is the best descriptive phrase for this kind of work. There is no desire or intensity of emotion. There is no mental idea of what things ought to be like. There is only a gentle radiance of enlightened awareness.

This energy, a gentle radiance of enlightened awareness, can do no harm and can only do good. It will not wind up a situation of conflict, but create a more mellow atmosphere in which it is easier for hot tempers to cool, for proud peoples to back down, for creative healing to happen. This gentle atmosphere can also do no harm to someone who is ill or in trouble. It helps the core self to come present.

In my trainings parents often ask about helping their children and sending them energy. Exactly the same rules apply. We must be non-judgemental, accepting and working from a point of alignment with essence.

A wonderful myth

As a final word in this chapter I would like to share a wonderful myth that may bring many of you comfort and hope. This myth comes from Tibetan Buddhism and tells us that there are three huge spiritual beings, three gods, who are always contemplating and thinking about humanity. Their sole purpose is to help us through our difficulties and pain.

They carry the unusual title of the Buddhas of Karma.

This myth says that these three beings have great power and sit in constant meditation, scanning the earth and humanity. They are studying our karma. They are contemplating the pain we experience as our negative energy patterns give way to the energy of our core selves and souls.

The Buddhas of Karma are perfectly aware of every nuance of human change as we try to integrate and work through our karma. They notice the moment that any one of us tries to melt through an old pattern and bring in love. Sometimes, when we are going through changes, our energies have a certain 'dance' to them and when the right moment comes, the Buddhas have the power to spin in extra liberating energy – and we may go through our change painlessly. They help us go through difficult changes without us having to feel that internal friction and psychological suffering.

The Buddhas of Karma do this work for humanity all the time. They might equally be called the Buddhas of

Grace. They cannot and need not be called into situations as they are always present and watching. It can do no harm to remember them.

9

You can make a difference

It is no longer secret

The aim of this book is to give you exercises that are easy to understand and easy to put into practice. There is no reason for this information to be shrouded in mystery or glamour. It is no longer necessary to join a secret organisation in order to learn these inner skills.

The fact that it is all so open and accessible is quite a change. Historically these techniques used to be secret and not so long ago people were burnt for even being interested in such subjects. I remember one Christian vicar telling me, with some satisfaction, that if I shared some of my ideas with his congregation they would very quickly have me out of the pulpit and on to a burning fire. Even today it is certainly not safe to discuss energy techniques in a fundamentalist religious society.

But the world has changed and is still changing. Whether it is the result of human evolution, part of a cosmic plan or just historical chance, the secret information of the past is now becoming public. Through modern science and new psychology we are also learning the mysterious beauty of sub-atomic life, and the continuum between matter and consciousness. Everything in the universe is made of energy and our consciousness is part of it. This is a new world view that enthusiastically recognises the depth and complexity and energies of the human psyche.

We, all of us, are beings of energy and of consciousness.

That is not a romantic or weird or mystic statement. It is a simple truth.

The historical change

As beings of energy and consciousness we experience many different moods and states, and we can choose to change these moods at will, changing our atmospheric influence on the world around us. We are definitely not victims of a cruel and predestined universe. We are co-creative actors affecting everything, materially and energetically. And, as creators, we can do good and we can do harm.

This ability to move matter and energy for good or for harm has worried many people in the past. It is under-standable why the 'mysteries' – teachings about how the inner world of energy and consciousness works – were kept secret and mysterious. Their teachers did not trust the majority of people to deal morally and ethically with the information.

There are still some who are frightened that people will use their understanding of energy for selfish reasons and I am sure they are sometimes right. Nevertheless, whether we like it or not, this information – once carefully guarded – is now public property. I am just a small part of an unorganised movement openly teaching it. Looking back, I did not originally make a conscious decision to do this teaching. I began it instinctively in response to people's needs and people immediately understood the information. I did not even think about secrecy or discretion. It seemed a perfectly normal thing to do.

What is fascinating to me is that this dramatic shift in our awareness of energy and energy work coincides with two other profound changes in human society. Alongside the new understanding of energy and consciousness, we also have for the first time a planetary village created by global telecommunications. Television and other satellite or on-line media have networked the whole planet, so that we are no longer separate communities but one global village.

The second profound change is that we are currently moving through a global crisis which touches everyone and everything. Living comfortable lives some of us may ignore the crisis, but it is obvious in the tens of thousands of children dying of hunger every day, in developing world debt which threatens to bring down the world economic system, in widespread city violence and in ecological pollution. These crises are global. In one form or another they ripple out to affect all of us.

Let me repeat this information so that it is absolutely clear. Simultaneously we have:

- a new and general awareness of consciousness and energy work;
- a global culture, a global village created by planetary telecommunications;
- a global crisis which affects all of us.

We have no choice but to help

It is startlingly clear to me that if we know about the world crisis and if we know about energy work, then we have no choice but to help. It almost seems to me as if it is part of some cosmic piece of education for us: here is the problem, here is the solution, get on with it.

Because of global telecommunications we are aware of the global crisis. Understanding the world of energies, we know that we are energetically connected to the crisis. And, therefore, we can do something about it! Most people feel impotent in the face of such huge problems, but energy work means that we can really help. Of course, first we have to rein in our own thoughtless behaviour and do nothing that adds to the weight of economic and ecological distress or social injustice – but then we can use our consciousness and ability to move energies.

Destructive actions begin in the hearts and minds of people. Whatever we do, therefore, to energetically enlighten our collective hearts and minds, works to the benefit of the whole situation.

We have to remember that energetically everything is interconnected and nothing is separate. Everything that has a similar vibration and quality is harmonically connected.

There are also the great clouds of emotional and mental energy created by humanity over thousands of years which influence and are influenced by all of us. War, for example, will never end completely until the great energy cloud of conflict and nationalism is dissipated and transformed. Starving children will never be fed until we all learn how to release and distribute our energy in a generous and caring way.

Negativity ripples through the whole system, but so do beauty and love. Every act of attitudinal love and beauty works to serve the whole. Every cleansing and blessing has its own small and beneficent effect on everything. One small energetic act of kindness may be enough to tip the scales in another situation ten thousand miles away.

Social activists have often been critical of the women

and men who live their lives in convents and monasteries. People who are politically active usually have little time for the hermit meditating in a mountain cave. But this ignores the energetic effect that these people are having. These isolated communities, wrapped in a rhythm of prayer and meditation, send great currents of love and help through the system. The monks who spend hours every day performing the classic practice of breathing in negativity and breathing out a blessing perform real service for all of us.

Every small act of generous energy, every little blessing and transformation, helps. Just being grounded and centred helps, because it radiates a calm which helps other people find their own centre.

There is no call upon you suddenly to change the whole of your life and become a renunciate saint. You just need to start with the little things at home and at work. Sometimes I think that the greatest energy work we can do is to smile at strangers on the street, and always give children our patient and warm awareness. These acts ripple through the world.

The end and the beginning

A healthy world needs empowered and benevolent human beings. It does not matter whether you clean streets or manage international companies, your real service comes from the attitude and energies you radiate.

Being calm and grounded, able to hold your centre when in crisis, you yourself become happier and more content, at the same time being a helpful model for those around you.

This book has, in fact, travelled quite a distance. It began with very personal things like grounding and personal protection. I next taught the techniques for cleansing and for blessing. You then learnt how to connect with your core and with the universal energy fields of love and beauty. Finally you saw how your attitudes and actions energetically serve the whole world.

From one perspective it is very ambitious, even romantic – the idea that you *can* change the world. From another perspective it is all very simple. It is just about living a better and more humane life, in action and in attitudinal energy, aware of the true realities.

I encourage you to begin this work, for it will serve you and it will serve all life.

You are sitting comfortably. You ground and monitor your breath. You are very patient. You wait until you feel yourself becoming calm. You switch on an inner philosophical smile and take yourself into a good mood. You sense the energies of the earth beneath you, holding you and making you feel safe and grounded. You are aware of and fully in your body. Your breathing is calm and regular. You feel relaxed, strong and attentive.

Staying perfectly comfortable, you expand your consciousness outwards. Gently you allow yourself to become aware of the suffering and pain that exists in the world. Particular people or situations may attract your focus. Your heart responds with sympathy and compassion to the suffering. You allow yourself to be aware of all human reality. You stay centred but fully present to human pain.

At the same time you begin to recognise the great currents of energy that flow through the body and atmosphere of the earth. You also open your awareness to the great waves of love and creativity that flow through the universe. The energies of the earth rise up into your body. The energies of the cosmos flow down through your crown. The essence of the sun radiates horizontally into you.

You have images of the people and beings whom you love. You think of situations that connect you with the sacred and you feel the beauty of life.

The situations of pain and suffering are indeed tragic, but the larger context is full of joy and strength.

Very tenderly, very carefully, you allow yourself to breathe in and absorb a small part of the pain. And then you breathe out a loving and sympathetic blessing into the pain. *I breathe in negativity. I breathe out blessing.*

You do not allow yourself to feel overwhelmed by the pain and suffering as you breathe it in. At the first sign of any overwhelming emotion you bring your focus purely back to the powerful love of the earth and universe. You breathe in negativity and you breathe out blessing. You do this for a minute or two.

You are connected to the great power of the earth and universe. Your own soul, your essence, is connected to this power and is subtly radiating through you. Your whole personality and physical body is comfortably feeling this wave-like radiation of blessing from you. You yourself receive the nurture from the blessing energy as you let it come through you and go to where it is needed.

You do this energy work for a while and then you stop.

You continue sitting quietly. You have no expectations and no impatience. You are wise and aware. You stay in the atmosphere, just observing, sensing and being. After a while it feels time to begin to move and get up.

Before you get up you monitor how you feel. Are you still grounded and breathing calmly?

Do you feel sensitive and exposed? If you feel exposed you use a simple technique of psychic protection, perhaps closing your energies down, like a flower at night closing its petals, or creating a bubble or flame or shield.

You feel strong and grounded. You have excellent awareness.

With no fuss, you continue with the work, pleasure and evolution of life.

Resources

Further reading

If you would like another perspective on protection and cleansing, there is one classic in this field which is old-fashioned but worth looking at. Dion Fortune's *Psychic Self-Defence* (Aquarian Books). If you are having particular trouble with relationships, then I recommend Phyllis Krystal's *Cutting the Ties that Bind* (Samuel Weiser).

If you want to explore more fully the art of being centred and inner dimensions, you might look at my own *Meditation in a Changing World* (Gothic Image). And if you want to explore further the whole issue of daily spiritual practice, then you might also look at my *First Steps: An Introduction to Spiritual Practice* (Findhorn Press).

Workshops

William Bloom conducts regular psychic protection and other workshops. For further information please contact Alternatives, St James's Church, 197 Piccadilly, London W1V 0LL. Tel: 0171-287 6711.

Cassettes

There are also two cassettes led by William Bloom that accompany this book:

Psychic Protection 1 Side A: Earthing, breath and safely in your body. Side B: Protection.

Psychic Protection 2 Side A: Connecting with the sacred. Side B: Disarming your 'enemy'.

Both tapes are available for £6.00 each from Alternatives, St James's Church, 197 Piccadilly, London W1V 0LL. Add £1.00 for posting and package within the UK. Please make cheques payable to 'Alternative Workshops'.

Index

Index

Index

pain, psychological, 140
peace, rules of intervention, 144
perception, 11–14
personal space, 72–3
personality, 75, 132–6, 139–40
photography, Kirlian, 9–10
pine, 67
plants, protective technique, 48
Pole Star, 105
pollution, 16, 61, 62
power animals, protective technique, 47–8
power plants, protective technique, 48
prayer, 54, 75, 76, 121, 130–1, 152
pregnancy, 23
protection techniques, 40–60
  asking for help, 48–9
  bubbles of protection, 42–4, 89
  the cloak, 46
  close down like a flower, 46–7
  coming from the countryside into the city, 56–7
  flame, 46
  knowing the enemies within, 58–60
  lead curtain, 47
  power animal, 47–8
  power plants, 48
  protecting someone else, 54–5
  protecting your home, 49–50
  protection through loving, 50–4
  shields, 45, 89
Psalms, 121
psychological safety, 2, 15
psychology, 133
psychotherapy, 109
pulse, awareness of, 32

rebirthing, 35
reincarnation, 76
relaxation, 40, 77
religions:
  angels, 128
  and evil, 113–14, 117
  fundamentalism, 86–7, 135, 148
  protective techniques, 48
  religious figures, 83
  superstition, 18
  symbols, 43
rest, 40
Roman Empire, 101
rules of intervention, 142–6

safety, psychological, 2, 15
sage, 67
salt, 67–8, 69, 89–91
sandalwood, 67
scents, cleansing techniques, 66–7
Scotland, 36
screaming, cleansing yourself, 71
self-control, 15, 22–3, 33–4, 92, 108
senses, 18–19
sex, 137–8
shaking, 70–2

PIATKUS BOOKS

If you have enjoyed reading this book, you may be interested in other titles published by Piatkus. These include:

The Afterlife: An investigation into the mysteries of life after death Jenny Randles and Peter Hough

Ambika's Guide To Healing And Wholeness: The energetic path to the chakras and colour Ambika Wauters

Art As Medicine: Creating a therapy of the imagination Shaun McNiff

As I See It: A psychic's guide to developing your healing and sensing abilities Betty F. Balcombe

Ask Your Angels: A practical guide to working with angels to enrich your life Alma Daniel, Timothy Wyllie and Andrew Ramer

At Peace In The Light: A man who died twice reveals amazing insights into life, death and its mysteries Dannion Brinkley with Paul Perry

Awakening To Change: A guide to self-empowerment in the new millennium Soozi Holbeche

Care Of The Soul: How to add depth and meaning to your everyday life Thomas Moore

Child of Eternity, A: An extraordinary girl's message from the world beyond Adriana Rocha and Kristi Jorde

Chinese Face And Hand Reading Joanne O'Brien

Colour Your Life: Discover your true personality through the colour reflection reading Howard and Dorothy Sun

Complete Book Of UFOs, The: An investigation into alien contacts and encounters Peter Hough and Jenny Randles

Complete Healer, The: How to awaken and develop your healing potential David Furlong

Contacting The Spirit World: How to develop your psychic abilities and stay in touch with loved ones Linda Williamson

Creating Sacred Space With Feng Shui Karen Kingston
Energy Connection, The: Answers to life's important
    questions Betty F. Balcombe
Feng Shui Kit, The: The Chinese way to health, wealth
    and happiness at home and at work Man-Ho Kwok
Full Catastrophe Living: How to cope with stress, pain
    and illness using mindfulness meditation Jon Kabat-
    Zinn
Handbook For The Soul: A collection of writings from
    over 30 celebrated spiritual writers Richard Clarkson
    and Benjamin Shields (eds.)
Healing Breakthroughs: How your attitudes and beliefs
    can affect your health Dr Larry Dossey
Healing Experience, The: Remarkable cases from a
    professional healer Malcolm S Southwood
Hymns To An Unknown God: Awakening the spirit in
    everyday life Sam Keen
I Ching Or Book Of Changes, The: A guide to life's
    turning points Brian Browne Walker
Journey Of Self-Discovery: How to work with the
    energies of chakras and archetypes Ambika Wauters
Journeys Through Time: A guide to reincarnation and
    your immortal soul Soozi Holbeche
Karma And Reincarnation: The key to spiritual
    evolution and enlightenment Dr Hiroshi Motoyama
Lao Tzu's Tao Te Ching Timothy Freke
Life Signs: An astrological guide to the way we live Julia
    and Derek Parker
Light Up Your Life: And discover your true purpose and
    potential Diana Cooper
Living Magically: A new vision of reality Gill Edwards
Many Lives, Many Masters: The true story of a prominent
    psychiatrist, his young patient and the past-life therapy
    that changed both of their lives Dr Brian L Weiss
Mary's Message To The World Annie Kirkwood
Meditation For Every Day: Includes over 100 inspiring
    meditations for busy people Bill Anderton
Message Of Love, A: A channelled guide to our future
    Ruth White

Strange But True? Stories of the paranormal Jenny Randles and Peter Hough

Supernatural Britain: A guide to Britain's most haunted locations Peter Hough

Teach Yourself To Meditate: Over 20 simple exercises for peace, health and clarity of mind Eric Harrison

Three Minute Meditator, The: 30 simple ways to relax and unwind David Harp with Nina Feldman

Time For Healing, A: The journey to wholeness Eddie and Debbie Shapiro

Time For Transformation, A: How to awaken to your soul's purpose and claim your power Diana Cooper

Toward A Meaningful Life: The wisdom of the Rebbe Menachem Mendel Schneersohn Simon Jacobson (ed.)

Transformed By The Light: The powerful effect of near-death experiences on people's lives Dr Melvin Morse with Paul Perry

Transform Your Life: A step-by-step programme for change Diana Cooper

Working With Guides And Angels Ruth White

Working With Your Chakras Ruth White

Yesterday's Children: The extraordinary search for my past-life family Jenny Cockell

Your Healing Power: A comprehensive guide to channelling your healing abilities Jack Angelo

For a free brochure with information on our
full range of titles, please write to:

Piatkus Books
Freepost 7 (WD 4505)
London W1E 4EZ